Psalm 91 Come into the Secret Place

Psalm 91 Come into the Secret Place

What Every Believer Needs to Know About the Most High

A DISCIPLESHIP TOOL

Dianne M. Hall

ISBN: 1541381866
ISBN 13: 9781541381865

To Tony
A Marine whom I met on a blind date,
this can be a very precarious step.
I am so glad God was in it, Mi Amor.

The Spirit and the bride say, "Come!"
And let the one who hears say, "Come!"
Let the one who is thirsty come;
and let the one who wishes take the
free gift of the water of life.

—REVELATION 22:17

Contents

Acknowledgments

MY THANKS BEGIN with the Lord Jesus Christ. My husband and I asked Jesus to come into our lives when we were twelve years into our marriage. Where would we be today without Jesus? We began seeking the Lord together and discovered an entirely new way to live—in God's Presence and in God's Word. We have been serving Jesus ever since. Father God has shown us His faithfulness and His transforming power in our entire family. When Jesus Christ comes into your life, He rescues you and sets you on a rock-solid foundation. I was living on sinking sand and believed that I was "just fine." Thank you, Lord Jesus, for all that you have done for me. Without You, I can do nothing. You chose me and you are my rescuing Savior day in and day out!

I want to thank my husband, Tony, who has been walking this journey of life with me for almost fifty years. I love you with all of my heart. I had no idea that our lives would have so much adventure. I am blessed that we can serve the Lord together and that God's not done with us, even at this season in our lives—no such thing as retirement! Let's name it re*fire*ment.

Jesus said, "Occupy 'til I come." In other words, keep working in the Kingdom until Jesus comes back to get you.

God gave us two sons and two daughters and then doubled the number when all four were married. Four young men, four young women—I count it double fruitfulness! I love each of you. Thank you for including us in your vacation plans. What a bonus! You inspire me as you follow Jesus and raise your children to love, serve, and fear the Lord.

Thank you to all who helped me with this book. Anna, you were the perfect choice to help with editing. I was blessed by your insight. Thanks.

To my daughters Laurie and Elizabeth who cheered me on to write this.

To Laura Gardiner who sent cards and verses to boost my writing endeavors.

To Shannon Shaffer, Dorothy Bauss, Kathy D, Barb Kacel, Deb Brown, Pastor Deb Kirgis, Sue Day, Kari Townsend, Beverly Hanners, Rich Vereeken—thanks for your encouragement.

To all those who prayed for me for this project—I would not have completed this book without your prayers. Thank you!

To Mark Gardiner, Ryan Johnson, Tom Townsend, and Dan Hanners for hours of technical help—I cannot thank you enough for your caring work.

Thank you, Pastor Cal and Sandy Garcia, for following God's call to Auburn Hills Christian Center. We thank God for the transformation in our lives during our time with you on staff. You inspired us to go and make disciples. You taught us that prayer is an essential part of any ministry effort. Our view of outreach ministry moved up several notches under your wise direction. We love and appreciate you and all that you are to the Body of Christ around the world.

We so appreciate all the pastors, the support staff, the board, and all our family at AHCC. We love you!

Thank you to Pastor Duane and Jeanie Vander Klok, our new pastors at Resurrection Life Church in Grandville, Michigan. We believe in the work of the Lord that you are doing in preaching God's Word to the local church and to the uttermost parts of the earth through television. Once again, God in His faithfulness has placed us in the midst of a loving, caring, and committed Body of Christ.

I have much to be thankful for!

Introduction

IT'S TIME FOR me to put into print what has been on my heart for many years: the awe-inspiring Psalm 91. It brings hope and blessing to my innermost being, and I want to pass that hope and that blessing on to you. Consider its promises and the blessings it contains for your life!

I began studying this psalm when I was a Christian schoolteacher. I taught it to my students. Over the years, God revealed more of its details to me. God's Word is always fresh for our lives. What we read yesterday will be enriched today. Like mown grass continues to produce healthy green shoots, the words of the Bible continue to produce life in our hearts even though we have read them before. That's why it's called the Holy Bible and why I keep going back for more!

I taught Psalm 91 in small ladies' groups and when I mentored new believers. I had a wonderful opportunity through my friend Andrea to speak to the ladies of Meadowbrook Christian Church at their sixth annual women's retreat. We had Saturday and Sunday to spend immersed in the Word of God at a lovely Bed and Breakfast, in Chesaning, Michigan. The women's leadership planned workshops for applying Psalm 91. They made quilt squares portraying images that represented what the Holy Spirit was showing them for their own lives. God's Word was unique to each woman!

In 2012, Tony and I accompanied Bob Hagerty and friend Pat Miller on a visit to the country of Myanmar, formerly known as Burma. The organization that Bob founded is called Mercy to the Children Myanmar, which sponsors four orphanages and Resurrection Life Church in Yangon (formerly known as Rangoon) the largest city in Myanmar. As we visited the children several times, we enjoyed worshiping with them. My husband and Bob baptized the children and taught them about communion. We visited the rice paddy owned by one of the orphanages. We learned about the pig farm they started. We heard about the peanut crop and the oil it produced. Our visit was fabulous! We loved meeting all the children. There are about one hundred orphans as of this writing.

Bob arranged for Tony and me to teach at Mingalarden Undergraduate School of Theology. I taught Psalm 91 in an all-day session. Pastor David Liam, the Bible school director, interpreted for me. What a joy and honor to meet this man of God and to share the Word of God with these precious students on the other side of the globe!

CHAPTER 1

Living by the Book

For the LORD **Most High** is awesome, the
great King over all the earth.

—PSALM 47:2

HAVE YOU EVER taken antibiotics for a sickness? Do you remember how sick you were before you started on the antibiotics? Do you recall that you wanted to start taking the medication as quickly as possible because you knew from past experience that your system would need a few doses before your symptoms began to disappear? Remember being amazed at how good you felt when the medicine started working? Did you also learn that if you stopped taking the medicine because you felt better, your symptoms would come back? All the medicine must be taken to fight against every germ causing the illness and to snuff it out.

The Word of God is like that antibiotic. It is powerful medicine for your spirit, soul, and body. If we apply it to our life situations, it will be the remedy we need when we take the full dose. What is the full dose? Take it daily. Sometimes we begin to get into the Bible and find out how comforting it is for our souls, and then we stop for some reason. But we learn that we cannot just take it when we start to feel better. We need to keep taking the daily dose.

Some years ago, my husband Tony had an infection in his leg. We didn't know that it was a puncture wound. It looked like water on the knee. When he tapped his knee with his finger, the swelling moved around. He was working at the Ford Tractor Plant in Romeo at the time and decided to have the plant's doctor take a look at it. He sent Tony immediately to a specialist, and the specialist sent him directly to the hospital. The infection was gaseous gangrene affecting the area from his knee to his ankle. The doctors opened up his leg with a six-inch incision. I was eight months pregnant, and the doctor quickly put me out of the room when he saw me there with Tony. We had no idea how dangerous this was. This type of gangrene progresses rapidly and causes tissue death. He was put in isolation immediately after I left the room.

Over several days, my husband received millions of units of penicillin. I knew that penicillin was a powerful antibiotic used to fight bacteria in your body, but millions of units seemed to be too much. Millions! I not only was worried about Tony's leg, but now I became concerned about the doctor. We were in a crisis, and we asked people to pray. God heard the prayers. He used this wise doctor to save my husband's leg.

In the same way that penicillin fought that deadly infection, the Bible is powerful medicine for our lives, and God is our wise doctor. Just as I needed to trust the doctor completely, I need to trust God completely. We cannot underestimate God's power to preserve us from everything in this world that would harm us. God saved Tony's leg and life through prayer and medicine—both were necessary. We needed to learn how to receive the blessings of God's promises.

I take large doses of the Book every day and I live by the Book. When I feel stress or fear coming upon me, I need mega doses of the Word of God. Many nights, hundreds of nights, I fall asleep meditating on the psalms especially Psalm 91.

Let's go to the foundation of this psalm, and along the way we will find out together why I consider Psalm 91 so valuable.

Who Wrote Psalm 91?

We're going to have to do some exploring to answer that question. King David wrote the majority of the psalms, but there are various other authors. Biblical scholars believe that Psalm 90 was written by Moses. Psalm 90 has a title: "A Prayer of Moses, the Man of God." The fact that Psalm 91 doesn't have a title and that it follows Psalm 90 links the two psalms together. Some scholars believe that Moses also wrote Psalm 91. We know that biblical scholars don't always agree, but as we examine Psalm 91 in this book, our foundation will be that Moses is the author. We will approach the psalm from that understanding and with that perspective.

Let's begin at the river and wind our way around to find the secret place of the Most High. Will you accompany me on this adventure? Come with me to the secret place. Shhh…there's peace, there's quiet, there's contentment here. You can almost hear the comforting sound of the river flowing.

> *There is a river whose streams make glad the city of God, the holy place where the Most High dwells.*—Psalm 46:4

Let's approach the throne of Most High together. There's assurance for you. You can hear the Most High God speak to you there. You'll love it! Psalm 91 describes a place where you can go to meet with God and experience the glory of His Presence.

> *He who dwells in the secret place of the Most High shall abide under the shadow of the Almighty.*—Psalm 91:1

- The King James Version (KJV) of the Bible uses the phrase "He who dwells in the secret place."
- The Good News translation says "Whoever goes to the Lord for safety."
- The Message Bible says *"You who sit down in the High God's presence."*
- The Complete Jewish Bible says "You who live in the shelter of Elyon."
- The Douay-Rheims Bible says "He that dwelleth in the aid of the most High."
- The New International Version (NIV) says "He who dwells in the shelter of the Most High."
- The Contemporary English Version (CEV) says to "Live under the protection of God Most High."

Which of these translations speaks to your heart?

I believe that God provides a place for us to go when life overwhelms us. When the path of life gets to be too much, too difficult, too busy, too stressful, too depressing, too sad, every person is invited to God's place. God provides a refuge for us. You can call it your safe place. You can call it your shelter. I like to call it my secret place. In this secret place, God delivers us, strengthens us, encourages us, and shows us who He is...and who we are. I am constantly discovering new things about God's goodness, mercy, and love when I go into this secret place. I am growing in my understanding of the Trinity: God the Father; God the Son, Jesus Christ; and God the Holy Spirit. I can be still here and know that He is God.

Because we believe that Moses is the author of Psalm 91, we are going to be looking at the life of Moses. You may be familiar with his story, or it may be new to you. The story of how God calls Moses to deliver the Israelites is found in Exodus 3:7. Moses is leading a flock of sheep in the back of the desert. God gets Moses's attention by drawing him to a bush that is burning but not consumed by the fire. As Moses turns to look closer, God calls his name: "Moses! Moses!" And Moses says, "Here I am." God speaks to Moses:

> The Lord said, "I have indeed seen the misery of my people in Egypt. I have heard them crying out because of their slave drivers, and I am concerned about their suffering. So I have come down to rescue them from the hand of the Egyptians and to bring them up out of that land into a good and spacious land, a land flowing with milk and honey… so now, go. I am sending you to Pharaoh to bring my people the Israelites out of Egypt."—Exodus 3:7–10

What an awesome verse! Moses is going to learn who this God is. Let's look at seven points that God is telling Moses.

1. **"I have seen the misery of my people."**
   - This is a God of compassion.
   - This God *sees* misery.
2. **"I have heard them crying out."**
   - This God *hears* His people crying out.

3. **"I am concerned about their suffering."**
    - This God *cares* about the suffering of His people.
4. **"I have come down *to rescue* them."**
    - This God has a rescue plan.
5. **"I am going *to bring them up* out of that land into a land flowing with milk and honey."**
    - This God *has a rescue plan* that is detailed.
    - He has *prepared a place* for His people.
6. **"So now, go."**
    - He commands Moses.
    - This God has *chosen a man* to work with Him in the rescue of His people. He has chosen Moses.
7. **"I am *sending you* to Pharaoh *to bring* my people the Israelites out of Egypt."**
    - This God commands with precise details.

At this point in the story, Moses reacts like many of us would react. He thinks of every reason why he cannot do what God asks. Moses reasons with God, and he has question after question: "Who am I that I should go to Pharaoh?" "What if the people don't believe me? What if the people don't listen to me?" God tells Moses His name: "I Am Who I Am." This is Yahweh. This is "the Lord, the God of your fathers—the God of Abraham, Isaac and Jacob." God shows him how to use the rod in his hand. Moses tells God that he is not an eloquent speaker. He is making excuses and complaining. Then Moses asks God to send someone else. Through this entire discourse, God instructs Moses and finally He tells him that Aaron, his brother, is coming to meet him, that they can go together, and that Aaron can speak for him. God has chosen Moses and He doesn't take no for an answer. Moses obeys God. It is a fascinating story, and things get worse before they get better. God has a plan, and it is going to take time to accomplish that plan.

Has that happened in your life? You feel alone. You feel that no one cares. You have excuses and complaints. Your circumstances get worse instead of better. God's timing is perfect, and He is working out a plan in your life. Like

Moses, you can go step by step and let God lead you through the plan. He may give you details, and He may not. God gives Moses more specifics:

> But I know *that the king of Egypt will not let you go unless a mighty hand compels him. So I will stretch out my hand and* strike *the Egyptians with all the wonders that I will perform among them. After that, he will let you go.*—*Exodus 3:19–20*

This God sees everything…He is omnipresent.
This God is all powerful…He is omnipotent.
This God knows the future…He is omniscient.

Moses did not know all that God would do through him. There were details that God didn't tell him, but Moses obeyed God one step at a time. God knows the outcome of your life. He sees the entire picture. He hears your cries, and he sees your suffering. Just as Moses had to trust God with every meeting he would have with Pharaoh, we have to trust God in our situations. God has a plan for your life.

Can you obey God like Moses—one step at a time?

Chapter 1
Prayer and Process

At the end of every chapter, we will use the ACTS model for prayer. Prayer is humbly talking to God. We adore, confess, give thanks, and intercede for others.

Acts

- **A is for adoration.** We enter the secret place of God, adoring Him. This is called worshiping and praising God.
- **C is for confession.** We confess and repent of sin.
- **T is for thanksgiving.** We give God thanks for all He has done for us. Psalm 68:19 (NKJV) tells us that the Lord daily loads us with benefits. There is always something to be thankful for!
- **S is for supplication.** This is where we petition God for the things we need, and we pray for the needs of others.

Adoration: Jesus, we adore you as King. We adore you because of who you are—God's Son. We worship you without asking for anything. We want to be close to you. You deserve our reverence.

Confession: I admit that I was fearful when Tony hurt his leg. When it comes to my family, I fear many things. Most High, I ask for forgiveness. I trust you with my life and the lives of my family.

Thanksgiving: Almighty God, I thank you that you saved Tony's leg. I thank you for showing me how powerful you are. Thank you for our salvation. Thank you for the written Word of God that we have.

Supplication: Holy Spirit of the living God, I ask you to come alongside us as we study the Word of God. Teach us how to be closer to the Most High than we have ever been before. We need you!

Process What You Have Learned

To process means to think about what you are thinking about. Have you noticed that we get so busy, we don't even have time to think? These pages at the end of every chapter are to help you slow down and meditate on what you have just read. You may have experienced a new revelation from God while reading. Be sure to write it down.

1. Moses saw a burning bush and thought about the fact that it was not burning up. He processed the event and decided to see why this was so unusual. God got his attention. Do you think we miss things because we don't take time to really look at them? When has God spoken to you to get your attention? How?

2. Take a few moments to be still—no distractions allowed. Listen for God's voice and His compassion as He speaks to you. What did He say to you?

3. A transformed life happens when we take the Word that we have heard or read and apply it to our own lives. How can you *apply* the story of Moses to your life?

4. When have you ever complained and made excuses to God?

5. Do you believe the statement that God sees your misery? What misery are you experiencing presently?

CHAPTER 2

God Wants to Live with You

> He who dwells in the secret place
> of the Most High shall abide under the
> shadow of the Almighty.
>
> —Psalm 91:1 (NKJV)

Let's take a closer look at the first verse of Psalm 91. It has seven key sets of words, which are highlighted and defined below.

HE

1. **HE**: The individual, every person—man or woman, young or old, children. Everyone is invited!

DWELLS

2. HE WHO **DWELLS**: In Hebrew, *yashab* means to dwell, to reside, to stay, to have your home, to inhabit, to settle. Dwell is a verb that means more than just passing by a place.

This reference means more than a casual visit. It means actually "living" in a place. A preparation has occurred. There is a choice to be made; a commitment is forming. God desires that we dwell in his Presence. He is asking us to live with Him. The wise say yes to God.

SECRET PLACE

3. HE WHO DWELLS IN THE **SECRET PLACE**: In Hebrew, the word for secret is *cether*. It means a covering, a hiding place, a shelter, a place of protection.

MOST HIGH

4. HE WHO DWELLS IN THE SECRET PLACE OF THE **MOST HIGH**: Most High: In Hebrew, *El Elyon* is one of the names of God.

Who owns the secret place? The verse says that the secret place is owned by the Most High. God invites us to come into this place. There is no other God higher than the Most High. The name Most High signifies power and might. He is above all gods.

Question: If this is God the Most High, does that mean there are lesser gods?

Answer: Yes, there are other gods—these are pagan and false gods.

The Egyptians worshiped false gods. People today believe in false gods. If there are lesser gods, I want the true God that is above all the false gods. Don't you? Why settle for "lesser"?

ABIDE

5. HE WHO DWELLS IN THE SECRET PLACE OF THE MOST HIGH SHALL **ABIDE**: In Hebrew, *luwn* means to lodge, stop over, pass the night, remain; to cause to rest or lodge.

Abiding is not a quick visit. The person isn't in a hurry. He is at rest. He is spending the night. He is remaining for a time. He has accepted God's invitation.

SHADOW

6. HE WHO DWELLS IN THE SECRET PLACE OF THE MOST HIGH SHALL ABIDE UNDER THE **SHADOW**: The shadow of the Almighty is a place of protection, a place of shade. This concept suggests closeness. You have to be close to someone to be under his shadow.

A few summers ago, my granddaughter Katelyn and I played a little game while we were on vacation. We were walking to the playground together, and we both noticed that there were shadows cast by the sun. Shadows tell us that a light source is near. We laughed as we chased and stepped on each other's shadows. I loved the game and the time to be lighthearted and free. God is a Father. Just as I loved playing with my granddaughter, I believe God loves to see us living under His shadow, enjoying our lives with Him. We enjoy His invitation.

ALMIGHTY

7. HE WHO DWELLS IN THE SECRET PLACE OF THE MOST HIGH
SHALL ABIDE UNDER THE SHADOW OF THE **ALMIGHTY**: In Hebrew,
the name of God is *Shadday*, which means most powerful. The first mention of
this name is in Genesis 17:1, where God appears to Abraham. God introduces
Himself with this name.

> *When Abram was ninety-nine years old, the Lord appeared to him and said, "I*
> *am God Almighty; walk before me faithfully and be blameless."*—*Genesis 17:1*

Let's go to the story of Moses coming out of the land of Egypt and see how all
this relates. God chooses Moses to deliver His people from slavery. There have
been ten plagues as judgments from God because Pharaoh would not let the
people go.

> *The Israelites set out from Rameses on the fifteenth day of the first month, the day*
> *after the Passover. They marched out defiantly in full view of all the Egyptians,*
> *who were burying all their firstborn, whom the Lord had struck down among*
> *them; for the Lord had brought judgment on their gods.*—*Numbers 33:3–4*

Did you catch that detail? The Egyptians were burying all their firstborn, from
Pharaoh's son to the firstborn of a slave girl. No one was safe except the Israelites.
The God of Moses gave Pharaoh nine warnings through plagues. Then came the
tenth plague: the death of the firstborn. Why wouldn't Pharaoh believe, even
though he saw God's power in nine previous plagues? The Bible tells us that God
hardened Pharaoh's heart. The full story is in the Book of Exodus, Chapters
1–15. The Lord gave Moses specific instructions:

> *Tell the whole community of Israel that on the tenth day of this month each man*
> *is to take a lamb for his family, one for each household…slaughter the lamb at*
> *twilight…then they are to take some of the blood and put it on the sides and tops*
> *of the doorframes of the houses where they eat the lambs…on that same night*
> *I will pass through Egypt and strike down every firstborn of both people and*

animals, and I will bring judgment on all the gods of Egypt. I am the Lord…no destructive plague will touch you when I strike Egypt.——Exodus 12:3–14

This is why He is called the Lord Most High and the Almighty. He hardened Pharaoh's heart to bring judgment on all the gods of Egypt. This was the first celebration of the Feast of Passover. The Israelites were rescued from slavery and set free.

God said, "This is a day you are to commemorate; for the generations to come you shall celebrate it as a festival to the Lord——a lasting ordinance."——Exodus 9:14

In Exodus 9:24–28, God makes it very clear:

Obey these instructions as a lasting ordinance for you and your descendants. When you enter the land that the Lord will give you as he promised, observe this ceremony. And when your children ask you, "What does this ceremony mean to you?" then tell them, "It is the Passover sacrifice to the Lord, who passed over the houses of the Israelites in Egypt and spared our homes when he struck down the Egyptians."

The Israelites did just what the Lord commanded Moses and Aaron to do in keeping the first Passover. The Feast of Passover is a celebration that Jewish people have observed for thousands of years in obedience to God's command. We have been privileged to celebrate Passover with our Jewish friends. Their hospitality to us has been a joy. They repeat this history lesson to their children every year and celebrate the story of Moses standing before Pharaoh. God moved mightily on their behalf and delivered them from their bondage as slaves in Egypt.

In these verses from Exodus 9, the Lord speaks of a time when the Israelites will enter the land that the Lord promised to give them. Do you know what land this refers to? It refers to the land of Israel. Israel became a nation in 1948. Since that time, this small nation has been fighting for its very existence. Jews are returning to this land from all the nations they were scattered to. This is one of the prophecies that are being fulfilled in our days.

[God said,] "I will signal for them and gather them in. Surely I will redeem them; they will be as numerous as before. Though I scatter them among the peoples, yet in distant lands they will remember me. They and their children will survive, and they will return. I will bring them back from Egypt and gather them from Assyria."—Zechariah 10:8–10

Moses said, "The Lord said to me: 'I will raise up for them a prophet like you from among their fellow Israelites, and I will put my words in his mouth. He will tell them everything I command him.'"—Deuteronomy 18:18

God told Moses that He was going to send a man like him. God kept His promise. Do you know the man who is referred to in this verse? The man is Jesus Christ. Jesus came to the earth in God's perfect time. He fulfilled this prophecy. Moses was sent by God to deliver, and his life points to Jesus Christ, who was sent by God to become The Deliverer. Everyone who believes in Jesus is delivered from slavery to sin. If you are addicted to drugs, you are a slave to drugs. If you are addicted to alcohol, you are a slave to alcohol. If you are addicted to lust, you are a slave to lust. Jesus came to set us free from every kind of slavery and every kind of bondage that we find in our lives.

This same verse is repeated in the New Testament in the Acts of the Apostles. The apostle Peter is speaking to a crowd of people who have witnessed a miracle. A man who was crippled from birth was carried to the temple gate every day to beg. On this particular day, Peter stops in front of the man and proclaims healing in Jesus's name, and the man stands up and walks, jumps, and praises God! Everyone knew the man because for many years they saw him whenever they passed the temple gate. Now the people are astonished and come running. This is what Peter said to these amazed people:

Men of Israel, why does this surprise you? Why do you stare at us as if by our own power or godliness we had made this man walk? The God of Abraham, Isaac and Jacob, the God of our fathers, has glorified his servant Jesus. You handed him over to be killed, and you disowned him before Pilate, though he had decided to let him go. You disowned the Holy and Righteous One and asked that a murderer be released to you. You killed the author of life, but God raised him from the dead. We are witnesses of this. By faith in the name of Jesus, this man whom you see and know was made strong. It is Jesus's name and the faith that comes through him that has given this complete healing to him, as you can all see.—Acts 3:12–16

Peter continues to talk to the people.

Now, brothers, I know that you acted in ignorance, as did your leaders. But this is how God fulfilled what he had foretold through all the prophets, saying that his Christ would suffer. Repent, then, and turn to God, so that your sins may be wiped out, that times of refreshing may come from the Lord, and that he may send the Christ, who has been appointed for you—even Jesus. He must remain in heaven until the time comes for God to restore everything, as he promised long ago through his holy prophets. For Moses said, "The Lord your God will raise up for you a prophet like me from among your own people; you must listen to everything he tells you. Anyone who does not listen to him will be completely cut off from among his people."—Acts 3:22–23

In order to come into the secret place, we must know Jesus. We established earlier that the secret lace belongs to the Most High. The following verses make it clear to us why we must know Jesus to enter this place. Jesus is God's Son. You cannot accept the Father and reject His Son.

Jesus said, "I and my Father are one."—John 10:30

Jesus answered: "I am the way and the truth and the life. No one comes to the Father except through me."—John 14:6

Jesus teaches us about the Father:

Then Jesus cried out, "When a man believes in me, he does not believe in me only, but in the one who sent me."—John 12:44

And beginning with Moses and all the Prophets, He explained to them what was said in all the scriptures concerning himself.—*Luke 24:27*

He said to them, "This is what I told you while I was still with you: Everything must be fulfilled that is written about me in the Law of Moses, the Prophets and the Psalms."—*Luke 24:44*

Philip found Nathanael and told him, "We have found the one Moses wrote about in the Law, and about whom the prophets also wrote—Jesus of Nazareth, the son of Joseph."—*John 1:45*

Jesus said, "If you believed Moses, you would believe me, for he wrote about me. But since you do not believe what he wrote, how are you going to believe what I say?"—*John 5:46*

He is the Most High God. He sent his Son to redeem us. Moses wrote about Jesus. The Feast of Passover points to Jesus. Jesus is called the Lamb of God. He was the lamb that was slain for all the sins of the world. He was crucified on a cross. Jesus's blood was shed. The blood of the lamb that was put on the doorframe of the house is a type of Jesus's blood. This story took place thousands of years ago, but it points to Jesus's sacrifice on the cross for us.

Prayer of Salvation

Have you ever asked Jesus to come and live in your heart? You can ask at this very moment in time.

If you have known Jesus and you have walked away from Him, you can come back to Him right now.

I invite you to pray this prayer:

Father, I believe that you gave your only Son, Jesus Christ, for me. I believe that Jesus came to earth, died on the cross, and was resurrected from the dead. He is alive and is seated with you

I need a Savior. I cannot save myself. I accept Jesus Christ as my Savior and I ask you to forgive me for every sin that I have ever committed.

I receive your salvation right now.

Come and live in my heart, Jesus. I believe that by your sacrifice on the cross, all my sins are forgiven, and the punishment for those sins is gone because you shed your blood for me.

My past is gone, and all things are new!

Thank you for saving me today, Lord Jesus!

Write today's date here_____.

Chapter 2
Pray and Process

Adoration: Most High, we worship you because you loved the world so much that you *gave* your only begotten Son that whoever believes in Jesus will not perish but will have life everlasting. You are always giving to us.

Confession: Lord Jesus, like Moses, I don't obey you right away. You command us to love people. I don't always do that. I confess my sin to you today. Thank you that you forgive me when I ask and cleanse me.

Thanksgiving: Almighty God, I thank you for my salvation. Thank you for setting me free from disobedience, lying, not loving people, and judging others. Thank you that I am free to serve you.

Supplication: Holy Spirit of the living God, visit us with revival in the United States. Bring us into unity in the Body of Christ. Deliver my family and friends from addictions to smoking, alcohol, drugs, lust, and porn. You are a holy God. Cleanse us, and bring conviction to our hearts.

Process What You Have Learned

1. What new thought did you receive while you were learning verse 1?

2. What words were new to you?

3. Did you memorize verse 1? Recite it and write it here.

4. How will you apply this verse to your life?

5. In your own words, express how you feel about the Most High.

CHAPTER 3

Say, Give Thanks, and Sing

I will say of the Lord,
he is my refuge, my fortress,
my God, in Him will I trust.

—*Psalm 91:2*

THIS SECOND VERSE changes dramatically. It is as if Moses realizes what a wonderful place the secret place is, and as he describes it in verse 1, he becomes filled with the knowledge of God. In that enthusiasm he writes verse 2 from his own point of view. Moses is speaking personally. The power of verse 1 is reaching his innermost being, and he begins to grasp the words in his spirit. The words are life to him! He wants all of Israel to respond to the Most High.

There are seven key sets of words to define and meditate on. They are highlighted below.

I

1. **I**: Moses is speaking.

SAY

2. I WILL **SAY**: To say is to speak with the mouth; to answer, to command, to tell, to call, and to promise.

Moses expresses his heart. This verse represents what it means to know the Most High in a personal relationship. I *say* who the Lord is to me personally.

If we have been transformed by coming into the secret place, our mouths will start speaking different things. What we *say* is very important.

> *For it is with your heart that you believe and are justified, and it is with your mouth that you profess your faith and are saved.—Romans 10:10*

LORD

3. I WILL SAY OF THE **LORD**: Lord is another name of God that we learn in this psalm. It is a title that shows surrender on our part when we call Jesus our Lord. Many people call Him Savior which means that they have accepted His sacrifice for the forgiveness of their sins. To call Jesus Lord means that not only have we received Him as our Savior, we have also surrendered our lives to Him and choose to follow where He leads us.

MY REFUGE

4. I WILL SAY OF THE LORD HE IS **MY REFUGE**: A refuge is a shelter from rain or storm or from danger or falsehood. Verse 2 says that when I need a refuge, I can say that God is *my* refuge. It's very personal.

A good example in nature is a turtle. He carries his shell wherever he goes. When danger comes, he withdraws into his shell, which is his refuge. God is always with us.

MY FORTRESS

5. I WILL SAY OF THE LORD, "HE IS MY REFUGE AND **MY FORTRESS**": A fortress is a fort, a citadel, a bastion, a castle; a strong place that cannot be conquered by the enemy.

When I need a strong place of protection from the enemy, God is *my* fortress. I *say* out loud that the Lord is my fortress. I can say, just as Moses did, that this strong place belongs to me—*my* fortress.

MY GOD

6. I WILL SAY OF THE LORD, "HE IS MY REFUGE AND MY FORTRESS, **MY GOD**": In Hebrew, God is called *Elohim*. When I need God, He becomes *my* God. It's very personal.

TRUST

7. I WILL SAY OF THE LORD, "HE IS MY REFUGE AND MY FORTRESS, MY GOD, IN WHOM I **TRUST**": To trust is to have confidence, to be bold, to be secure, to feel safe.

Because of all the things that Moses believes in his heart, he then says, "He's the One I am going to trust!" Moses is facing many things, and all his trust is in God helping him in his circumstances. The Most High is overshadowing Moses.

Do you see how close God has come to you as you've meditated on these words? We have memorized them, and we didn't even have that as our goal.

We have a trust in him that we didn't have before. We are learning and leaning on God and discovering the Lord in a new way! We see that we belong to God and He belongs to us. We dwell with God, and He dwells with us. Where are we? We are in the "secret place of the Most High."

Here's a glimpse into the story of Moses and Aaron meeting with the elders of the Israelites.

Moses and Aaron brought together all the elders of the Israelites, and Aaron told them everything the LORD had said to Moses. He also performed the signs before the people, and they believed. And when they heard that the LORD was concerned about them and had seen their misery, they bowed down and worshiped.—Exodus 4:29–31

This is a precious verse. Look at all that happened in this meeting. Look what God had done!

- Moses told the elders everything that the Lord had said to him.
- Moses performed the signs that God had shown him.
- The elders believed.
- They learned from Moses that God was concerned about them.
- They learned that God had seen their misery.
- They bowed down and worshiped God.

Many people today need to know that God is concerned about them and sees their misery. This ancient message is also for you today. When you know that God is aware of your troubles and that He cares, do you want to believe in Him? The enemy of your soul, Satan, wants you to believe that God doesn't care about you. But he is the father of lies.

Jesus Becomes My Savior

My husband Tony and I lived in Romeo, Michigan, for fifteen years when our children were growing up. Romeo is a farm community about forty miles north of Detroit. We lived in the country in a small subdivision on 1.75 acres. We had farmland all around us. Country living is different, and it took getting used to. But I found that when I had adjusted to life in the country, I didn't want to go back to city life. What a blessing it was from the Lord to raise our children in this country setting. This was a wonderful period in our lives. I was a stay-at-home mom, and I kept busy. I belonged to the Newcomers Club, a bridge club, a quilt club, and a pinochle club. I was a hostess for the Romeo Historical Society's annual house tours.

My husband worked for the Romeo Tractor Plant. He coached Little League baseball, played in a baseball and golf league, and became a volunteer fireman for the Bruce Township Fire Department. Every Labor Day, Romeo celebrated the Peach Festival, and Tony marched in the honor guard in the festival parade. Some years we entered floats in the children's parade. We won a trophy one year for our neighborhood entry. There were various games during the festival. Our son Chris and daughter Laurie won trophies in the peach-pie-eating contest. The trophy for this event was gold and about twelve inches high, and on the top of the trophy was a pig! This is how I think of America—family get-togethers, parades, patriotism, churches, being involved in the local community, knowing your neighbors. What fun we had in this community as a family of six!

Little did we know then that our lives were about to change forever. It was in this community, in a little country church up the road, that I gave my heart to Jesus. We had just come through a very difficult time. I was pregnant with our fourth child. Tony almost lost his leg from a bad infection. I was asking, "What's this life all about, anyway?" Those were my thoughts as I mowed the grass on our riding mower. I could feel desperation and depression settling into my mind. Our lives can be busy and full, and yet there is a hole inside of us, a void that needs to be filled.

Two years prior, a neighbor had invited me to a prayer group in her home. At that time in my life, I didn't respond to her invitation. I told myself I didn't need a prayer group. Now, two years later, I knew I needed something. I made a call to Donna Hobbs to ask her if I could come to that prayer group. She was glad that I called and said to me, "We don't have that prayer group anymore. We're going to this little church up the road. Would you like to go with us?"

My thought now was "I have to find God." I never went to other churches, ever—only Catholic churches. But I went to this little church with her the next Sunday.

The Holy Spirit was preparing my heart, and I didn't know it. People were praying for me, and I didn't know it. God was about to show me that He saw my misery and that He cared about me. All I knew was that I was desperate.

At this church, they did things very differently from what I was used to. They asked us if we wanted to raise our hands and receive Jesus in our lives. I sat there and thought, "I know Jesus. After all, I go to church every Sunday. I always have. I was baptized as a baby. I went through Confirmation in eighth grade." What were these people talking about?

I went home, and as I stood at the kitchen sink, doing the dishes, my mind whirled with songs from that little church. They called it praise and worship. I can still see the wooden board where they listed the songs that they would sing that morning. It was all new to me, and I didn't like it, probably because it was different from what I was used to. The fact that I didn't like it did not prevent the music from surfacing inside me when I got home, though. This was all so strange. I didn't like it, and I did like it!

So the next Sunday I went to this little church again. I didn't like it again, but I did. I came back to my kitchen sink and thought about the Word that was preached. I thought about it all week long. I decided that next time I went, I would raise my hand to ask Jesus into my heart. But next Sunday, the strangest thing happened at church. My hand didn't go up. Then one Sunday, Pastor

Halquist asked people to come to the altar if they needed healing. I believed in healing and miracles, and I needed healing for my skin. I had been diagnosed with psoriasis at age nineteen. Now there was no hesitation. My feet carried me right down to that altar. Nothing could have held me back. This is how I know that the Holy Spirit was convicting my heart. The Bible says that the Holy Spirit draws us to Jesus. We have to yield to that drawing.

> [Jesus said,] "When the Advocate comes, whom I will send to you from the Father—the Spirit of truth who goes out from the Father—he will testify about me."—John 15:26

I wanted to raise my hand—that was in my mind. The Holy Spirit testifies to our *spirit* about Jesus. The Holy Spirit was ministering to my spirit. As soon as Pastor Halquist placed his hands on my head to pray a healing prayer over me, these words came out of my mouth—out of my spirit: "Jesus, I accept you as my personal Savior." I knew that if I was the only person who had sinned and needed to be cleansed, Jesus still would have died for me. The Holy Spirit had to prepare my heart to receive Jesus. My mind told me I didn't need Jesus and that I was fine. But my heart knew that Jesus was what I was longing for to fill the void in my life.

Just as all conversions to Jesus are awesome, my conversion to Jesus Christ held to that truth. In Luke 15:10, the Bible tells us that the angels rejoice over one sinner who repents. Well, that day I rejoiced with the angels, because I was changed at that very moment. I had never asked Jesus to live in me. Jesus was on the outside of me, and what I had was an outside religiosity. Asking Him to come into my heart changed everything. I didn't know that you could ask Jesus to live inside of you. I received a hunger for the Word of God that I had never known before. I'd never read the Bible. Now I couldn't put the Bible down. The Lord also gave me understanding as I read the Bible. It opened up to me, and I was amazed. It seemed as though a veil was lifted off my eyes and my mind.

I always prayed and went to church but I began attending church every Sunday morning, every Sunday night, and every Wednesday evening. I simply couldn't get enough of the preaching of the Word of God. Some people call this experience "finding religion." For me, it was finding a relationship with Jesus. I had religion before this, and it wasn't satisfying. I had an emptiness that only

God could fill. I was hungry to hear the Word of God. Jesus *is* the Word of God and He was becoming real to me!

I remember thinking, "I can't wait until I can *say* that I've known the Lord for a long time." What I learned, though, is that people sometimes stop growing. We have to be lifelong learners. Jesus is looking for fruit. He even said that we would know His disciples by their love, not by their years. Christians can cease to grow and produce fruit in their lives. Jesus wants our lives to have love, joy, peace, long-suffering, kindness, goodness, faithfulness, gentleness, and self-control— the qualities that compose the fruit of the Spirit. How is your fruit these days? Are you filled with peace and joy? Are you kind to your family? Do you find yourself filled with a love for people? Are you able to control your anger and what you speak? Would your family say that you are different now that you have the Lord in your heart? Jesus taught His disciples in John 15:16–17:

> *You did not choose me, but I chose you and appointed you so that you might go and bear fruit—fruit that will last. Then the Father will give you whatever you ask in my name. This is my command: Love each other.*

Having four children, I often found my quiet time in the bathroom, where I could close the door and open the window and talk to God. I was just learning how to read the Bible on a daily basis. I had never read it through. I had a Bible that I had kept from our religion classes at Catholic Central High School in Grand Rapids. I never realized the richness of the Bible and that I would delight in reading it.

I grew in my Christian walk. One Sunday at Mass, there was a visiting priest who encouraged us to read our Bibles. I had never heard this before. Here was this priest giving details on how to work it out in your life so that you could read the Bible. "Don't place your Bible on your nightstand. You will not pick it up and read it. It will just collect dust. If you put your Bible on your pillow, you will have to pick it up to get into bed. Your Bible will be in your hand, and you will open it up and read it." Sure enough! I began placing my Bible on my pillow and I developed the habit of reading it every day.

As time went on, I learned how to walk with the Lord day by day. I was like a baby learning to walk. Sometimes I fell down, but I got up and tried again. One evening, the Lord showed me something very special and personal. I went into the living room and sat down. This was unusual for me, because we rarely used this room except on special occasions. We spent the bulk of our life as a family in the kitchen, family room, and outside. But I felt called to the living room. I felt the presence of the Lord. I had an impression that Jesus was sitting in one of our living room chairs. (This was not an open vision.) He was waiting for me to sit with Him and talk. He showed me how I was going into all the other places of the house, but I was not coming into the living room and sitting down with Him because of my busyness. Jesus was there, and I was ignoring Him! That mental picture of Jesus sitting and waiting for me changed my devotional life. I began spending time with Him every night before I went to bed. We enter the secret place when we spend time with the Lord and when we arrive at His throne room of peace.

Jesus wants that friendship with all of us. He wants that closeness—we call it intimacy. He doesn't want to be a guest or an acquaintance. He wants to live with us and become our close friend. We seem to be oblivious to this truth: He chose us before we ever thought of choosing Him! He begins to teach us to follow Him. He begins to change our hearts.

For the mouth speaks what the heart is full of.—Matthew 12:34b

What we say is so important. I can specifically remember once bumping my head really hard as I was getting in our big van, and I did not swear. Old speech in me was gone, and I had new speech! A curse was not in my heart—Jesus was in my heart. The Spirit of God will show you that your life is being transformed. The conviction of how we speak comes from the Holy Spirit. Yield to Him. The Bible teaches us in Proverbs 18:2 that life and death are in the power of the tongue. We begin to desire to speak words of life to all those around us at home or at work. We don't want to speak death any longer. The Holy Spirit changes us as we yield to the conviction that He brings.

As I read and meditate on Psalm 91, my confidence in God grows. I have a new resolve to spend time in the Bible and to talk to God in prayer. I am *saying* that He is my Lord and Savior. I am *thanking* Him for all that he has done in my life. I am applying the words found in the Bible and my speech is becoming different. What I say is important to me. I am *singing* praises to Him. My life has become full of newness!

Chapter 3
Pray and Process

Adoration: Most High, I love you because…you are my God, my Creator, my Lord, my salvation. (Add your praises.)

Confession: Lord Jesus, I have fallen short…I have been saying the wrong things. Forgive me. I want to speak the right kind of things to myself and my family and friends. (Confess your sins to God.)

Thanksgiving: Almighty God, I thank you that I am learning to trust you. I can come to you and you can give me refuge. You can be my fortress. You can be my personal God and Savior. Thank you for changing my circumstances. (Add your thanks.)

Supplication: Holy Spirit of the living God…I pray for America, that you will help us be a godly nation again. We need you in our country. We have been so far away from you. (Add your prayers for family, work, school, and friends.)

Process What You Have Learned

1. Can you recite verses 1 and 2 by heart? Can you write them by heart?

2. What would you *say* about the Lord to someone?

3. What is your favorite song that you enjoy singing to the Lord?

4. List all the things that you are thankful to the Lord for. There is *always* something to be thankful for.

5. What circumstances are you going to trust the Lord with?

CHAPTER 4

Surely! A Word of Hope

Surely, he will save you from
the fowler's snare and from
the deadly pestilence.

—PSALM 91:3

PSALM 91:3 GOES back to the third person ("Surely *He* will save"). This changing back and forth is important, and to me, it signals that Moses is teaching the people. He wants them to know that what God did for him, God would do for all the people. Moses encourages them to believe the truth about the Most High. In this verse, Moses is speaking *about* God. There are seven key words that we will look at closely.

SURELY

1. **SURELY**: This is an adverb meaning in a sure manner; safely, confidently, certainly, without danger or risk of injury or loss. Surely is used three hundred times in the NIV.

This word has blessed me beyond measure, as I think of God wanting to rescue his children surely—a sure thing. Not maybe, or sometimes, but *surely*. This is like a guarantee—to assure, to promise something, or to make something certain. Here are some other "surelys" that have helped me realize God's goodness.

Surely goodness and mercy shall follow me all the days of my life.—Psalm 23:6 (KJV)

What a promise!

> *Surely, Lord, you bless the righteous; you surround them with your favor as with a shield.*—Psalm 5:12

God favors you!

> *The boundary lines have fallen for me in pleasant places; surely I have a delightful inheritance.*—Psalm 16:6

You *have* an inheritance, and it's delightful!

> *Surely God is my help; the Lord is the one who sustains me.*—Psalm 54:4

You are not alone—God will help you!

HE

2. SURELY **HE**: He is the Most High.

SAVE/DELIVER

3. SURELY HE WILL **SAVE**: To save or deliver means to snatch away, to rescue, to save, to recover; to be torn away; to deliver from enemies or troubles or death; to deliver from sin and guilt; to be plucked out.

God called Moses to be the deliverer of His people. With this call, God was asking Moses to snatch the Israelites away from their enemies. Moses is called to rescue them from the bondage of slavery. He fervently wants the people to believe in the Most High.

YOU

4. SURELY HE WILL SAVE **YOU**: Moses is making it personal for them as he teaches: "He did it for me [Moses], and He will do it for you."

FOWLER

5. SURELY HE WILL SAVE YOU FROM THE **FOWLER**: A fowler is one who sets a snare in place. He is the trapper, the bait-layer. A fowler is a type of Satan, our enemy, who sets snares to trap us.

SNARE

6. SURELY HE WILL SAVE YOU FROM THE FOWLER'S DEADLY **SNARE**: A fowler's snare is a bird trap. Snares can also be calamities or plots set against people.

We are assured that God will deliver the righteous from the enemy's plan of evil. The snare is a trap that wicked men, fallen angels, and demons set for the righteous. How are we made righteous? Jesus made us righteous when He shed His blood on the cross. Because of Jesus's sacrifice, we are in right standing (righteous) with the Most High.

> *My dear children, I write this to you so that you will not sin. But if anybody does sin, we have an advocate with the Father—Jesus Christ, the Righteous One.—1 John 2:1*

Applying the Word

I know that I am not the only one who needs prompting in how to apply the Word of God to my everyday life. The Lord is with me, and prayer is essential, but on the other side, the enemy comes to steal, kill, and destroy. He is always setting snares for us. I need to be reminded daily to pray, love, and serve, and to be watchful of the enemy.

Once I was in the hospital for a routine outpatient colonoscopy. The doctor removed some polyps, a rescue of sorts, and I thanked God for it. The doctor did not want to take any chances that I would bleed, so she decided to keep me overnight in the hospital for observation. The potassium in my body was totally depleted. As they put the potassium in my arm through an IV, I felt my entire arm burn like it was on fire. I called the nurse. She was able to turn down the amount of potassium that was going into my arm, and the burning sensation lessened. I was wide awake through the night. Then the nurse came to check on me and found me sitting up in bed. She called me Shirley. I said to her, "My name's not Shirley," wondering how the nurse could get my name wrong. After all, she had my chart.

When the nurse left my room, I began thinking about her calling me by that name, and my mind went to Psalm 91:3 and the word "surely." I giggled to myself because I knew I needed a reminder of God's promises. I was prompted to pray that verse. I got out of bed to walk around the unit. Was there a "snare" here? I was walking and praying instead of worrying, fretting, or complaining. We all know that with any procedure, even something routine, there can be complications. My father survived bypass heart surgery but died during a routine operation ten years later. Doctors didn't know then what they know now about blood thinners. My mother was heartbroken to lose my dad at the age of seventy-one in a small operation.

Of course, I was thinking about all that when I was admitted to the hospital. But as I prayed, I became peaceful. I resisted worry and fear, and they were gone. God was with me in that hospital room, delivering me from the fowler's snare.

DEADLY PESTILENCE

7. SURELY HE WILL SAVE YOU FROM THE FOWLER'S DEADLY SNARE AND FROM THE **DEADLY PESTILENCE**: Deber in Hebrew which means pestilence or plague.

> *By day the Lord went ahead of them in a pillar of cloud to guide them on their way and by night in a pillar of fire to give them light, so that they could travel by day or night. Neither the pillar of cloud by day nor the pillar of fire by night left its place in front of the people.—Exodus 13:21–22*

> *Then the angel of God, who had been traveling in front of Israel's army, withdrew and went behind them. The pillar of cloud also moved from in front and stood behind them, coming between the armies of Egypt and Israel. Throughout the night the cloud brought darkness to the one side and light to the other side; so neither went near the other all night long.—Exodus 14:19–20*

These have always been some of my favorite Old Testament verses. I imagine when the Egyptians came after the Israelites. The fire of God's Presence lit up the camp of the Israelites, but on the side of the Egyptians, it looked like a dark, ominous cloud. I love this—with God on our side He causes us to see things differently! God separated the Israelites from their enemies and wouldn't let them come near.

In the *Zondervan Pictorial Encyclopedia of the Bible Volume 4,* we are given insight on the word *pestilence* and what it meant to the people. The Hebrew word for pestilence is found forty-nine times in the Old Testament. It occurs in company with such words as famine, blood, wild beasts and death. The first occurrence of the term is in connection with the plagues on Egypt (Ex. 5:3, etc). Later it was threatened on Israel if they disobeyed God (Lev 26:25, etc). Pestilence was so feared by the people that Solomon prayed for relief from it before it should come on Israel (1 Kings 8:37). Relief could come only when the people repented, humbled themselves, and sought God's face (2 Chr. &:13,14). This would indicate that pestilence came as a punishment on Israel for her disobedience and rebellion against God (Hab. 3:5).

The word *pestilence* is found in the New Testament, also, and is a word used by Jesus to foretell the events and occurrences before His return to the earth in the last days (Matt. 24:7; Luke 21:11).

Ask yourself if you could have this assurance in your heart: Because I know the Most High, I can be as safe in the middle of a battle in wartime as I am safe in bed in my home.

We don't have to fear if we live under the shadow of the Most High.

The Most High keeps me safe!

Chapter 4
Pray and Process

Adoration: Most High, I love you because I have seen your deliverance in my life. I worship you because I know that you love me and have my best interests in your plans for my life. I know that you keep me safe. (Add your worship.)

Confession: Lord Jesus, I have fallen short because I worry instead of trusting you. I am full of fear instead of faith. Forgive me. Father, I need to forgive _____. He/she really hurt me. Help me to forgive this person. I want to forgive the church people who hurt me. I stopped going to your house because of what they did to me. Help me, Lord.

Thanksgiving: Almighty God, I thank you for building my faith during trials. I am learning to trust you, and it makes me joyful to know that my faith is stronger.

Supplication: Holy Spirit of the living God, I need you to show me how to live this life in the spirit and not in the flesh. There are things happening at work and home, and I need your wisdom. Help me remain calm and peaceful through it all.

Process What You Have Learned

1. Has God delivered you from any snares or any kind of pestilence in the past? When has He kept you safe?

2. Do you need the Lord to deliver you from something in your life right now? Does a friend or family member need the Lord to deliver them?

3. What do you believe about the devil? Do you think he is real? Does he have more power than the Most High?

4. Can I be as safe in the middle of a wartime battle as I am safe in my own bed in my home right now?

The Names of God

I will be glad and rejoice in you;
I will sing the praises of your
name, **O Most High.**

—Psalm 9: 2

Don't you love it when someone uses your name to address you? You feel so special that someone cared enough to remember your name. There is value attached to our names. God's names are very significant. In chapter 1, we looked at the names of God. I want to go a little deeper in this chapter to explain the importance of the names of God. At different times in our lives, God will reveal Himself to us with one of His names. These revelations teach us God's character. The Most High wants you to know who He is!

These are the names of God used in Psalm 91:1–2.

- El Elyon—Most High. This title stresses God's strength, his sovereignty, and his supremacy.
- Almighty—El Shaddai is the all-sufficient God. In Hebrew, the word *shadaim* indicates that God is "enough."
- Lord—Jehovah.
- My God—Elohim.
- Alpha and Omega (Rev. 1:8; 26).

By experience and study, we learn that God has awesome names with great meaning for us personally. For example, Moses became acquainted with the Most High

God, and He takes Moses through the ten plagues. The plagues did not harm the Israelites. Next He protects Moses and the people as He leads them out of Egypt into the wilderness and then to another land that He has prepared for them. Psalm 91 reveals the man Moses coming to the great knowledge of who El Elyon is. Moses wants the people to grasp what he has learned about the Most High. Moses is encouraging his people in difficult circumstances. God's name brings comfort.

Through our trials and difficult circumstances, we come to know the Lord by one of His names. When I came to Father God through Jesus, and when I was drawn by the Holy Spirit, I thought that I would be protected from trials in life. I quickly learned otherwise. God takes us through life trials and protects us in them. We don't escape; we go through and come out better on the other side with more knowledge of who God is. He is training us to be overcomers. I learned to trust God. I am still learning to trust Him more and more. I haven't arrived at perfect trust. The very struggles that we encounter are what God uses to draw us to Himself. He does not, however, use evil against us. The devil uses evil against us, and when he does, God turns that evil so that it works for good in our lives.

Are you struggling? You are not alone. We feel alone in our struggles and distresses, but God is with us.

A Call to Missions?

My husband and I had the most delightful surprise in regard to Tony's American heritage. We were living in a flat on the northeast side of Detroit, and Chris, our firstborn, was a baby. This was a long time ago, before personal computers. I will never forget the occasion. His beloved Aunt Beth had come to visit us all the way from Florida. She was a link to his father's side of the family. Tony's father was killed in World War II three months before Tony was born. He was born on his father's birthday. As we were visiting, Aunt Beth presented us with a large piece of paper that was folded into four large sections. We opened it up and found a family crest drawing, and a family tree dating all the way back to 1816! We were happy to receive it. We filed it away.

It is amazing how God guides our lives. This guidance unfolds over time. Fast-forward about ten years. We had committed our lives to the Lord Jesus and were attending a church that was very missions oriented. We went on several missionary trips. I accompanied my good friend Kathy on a trip to Guatemala. This was pretty exciting because I had never been out of the country. I had never been separated from my husband. I found that I loved to travel and meet new people. This trip was quite an excursion because we had to take a twelve-hour road trip by van from Guatemala to Honduras with four adults and three children. In a third world country, that equates to no restaurants and no bathrooms on the way. We packed food and toilet paper and a change of clothes, and away we went.

Our next trip, when my husband and I went to Honduras on a singing tour, was equally challenging. We were part of a group of six adults and twenty-six students of high-school age. Do you know how much luggage we needed to shuffle around for thirty-two of us? But it was another awesome trip as the students sang and gave their testimonies.

My husband led a work team to help build an orphanage and church in Honduras in a place called Valle de Angeles, the Valley of the Angels. We got out the family tree again and were amazed to find that there were missionaries in Tony's family line—one, two, three generations in Burma. How excited we were to know this information that seemed to have been hidden from us for a time. It had new value to us because our lives were transformed—we had a relationship with Jesus now! He says, "Come follow me."

We were praying and asking God about becoming missionaries. Was He calling us? Was He leading us? It seemed like a far-out idea. Then, on one of our missionary trips, my husband came to me and said, "I believe we should definitely pursue the mission field." I had to process this, so I went up on the roof of the Mayan Hotel in Tegucigalpa. I was struggling. It is one thing to go on a short mission trip for a week or two, knowing that you are going home soon. You know that you will be returning to normal life with all the amenities of your home, your family, your car, your job. It is an entirely different thing to quit your job, sell your home, and move to another country to serve God and His people and learn a new language too.

For years, I sat in church services and heard missionaries tell their stories about how they crated their belongings, and off they went to serve in Africa and other faraway lands. I loved hearing their stories! I sat in the pew and said to myself, "I could never do that." It wasn't me saying no to God (or was it?). Actually, it was unbelief. But on this rooftop, out in the open, on a beautiful tropical blue-sky morning in a foreign country, I called out to God. I felt the Lord answered my groanings by showing me an ant carrying a piece of popcorn. My eyes focused on that ant, and I saw that the popcorn was much bigger than the ant. Yet it appeared that the ant carried the burden effortlessly. I knew the Lord was whispering to my heart, "You think you can't do it, but you can carry more than you think, because I am with you."

There is a verse that I quoted all the time to my elementary students when they said "I can't": "I can do all things through Christ who strengthens me" (Phil. 4:13). Now it was time for me to practice what I preached.

We started the process. Day by day we moved toward being missionaries. Many decisions later, we said good-bye to our two oldest children, Chris, twenty-two years old, and Laurie, twenty years old and newly married. A month after her wedding, we headed to Latin America with our youngest two children, Jason, fourteen, and Elizabeth, twelve. We sold our house. Our belongings, including a car, were packed in a large container that would travel by truck, train, and ship to a port in Honduras. Nothing is impossible with God—only believe.

We moved to the capital city of Tegucigalpa, Honduras, Central America, and became part of a missionary team. We were involved in a local church, humanitarian aid, medical missions, a Bible school ministry, construction projects, home groups, homeschooling, preaching in small churches, Saturday school (like Sunday school) in the Valley of the Angels, dental missions, and baptisms that were such a joy! On the mission field, the needs are always plentiful. (Whew!)

Because we were involved in so many things, I cried out in the secret place for strength and wisdom. Jesus revealed Himself to me by another one of his names. Alpha and Omega are the first and last letters of the Greek alphabet. This name of God comes from the Book of Revelation:

> *"I am the Alpha and Omega," says the Lord God, "who is, and who was, and who is to come, the Almighty."—Revelation 1:8*

He said to me: "It is done. I am the Alpha and the Omega, the Beginning and the End. To the thirsty I will give water without cost from the spring of the water of life."—Revelation 21:6

I would pray, "Lord, you are the beginning of my day and the end of my day. Lord, you are at the beginning of my night, and you will be at the end of my night." Of course, He was in the middle too! I had to personalize the verse because it brought me great comfort. "You are my Alpha and my Omega, Lord Jesus," I would say. He would tell me, "I am changing you just by you being here." He changes us one day at a time into His image as we serve Him. We cannot do the changing ourselves.

When we accept Jesus as our Savior, He comes to live inside us. We let Jesus come to the forefront of our lives as in the illustration.

When we die to ourselves, there is more of the life of Jesus in us.

For you died, and your life is now hidden with Christ in God.—Colossians 3:3

I have been crucified with Christ; it is no longer I who live, but Christ lives in me; and the life which I now live in the flesh I live by faith in the Son of God, who loved me and gave Himself for me.—Galatians 2:20 (NKJV)

Christ in you the hope of glory.—Colossians 1:27

So if the Son sets you free, you will be free indeed. —John 8:36

- The image of God, the image of Jesus, increases in us as we grow in the things of God.
- Life becomes more of Jesus and less of us.
- Jesus wants to live and minister through us.
- We become Jesus's hands, His feet, and His mouth speaking words of life to others.

When we *live* in the secret place, it means that we go to God first when "life happens." We don't go to him as a last option because we have tried everything and it hasn't worked. We go to Him *first*.

On the mission field, when we were at church one Sunday, robbers entered our home. On another afternoon, our neighbor's house, which was adjoined to ours (they were our landlords), was robbed when we were right in the house. I heard gunshots! I dropped to my knees and prayed. God kept us all safe.

We can become fearful through these events, or we can go to the secret place and ask God to help us. God knows everything. He is never surprised, because He has foreknowledge—He is omniscient. He lives in the eternal time zone. We live in the temporal time zone. We do not have foreknowledge. He knows what we need.

I hope that you will choose God first right now and come into the secret place and meet God there. He will speak to you and show you how to cling to Him. He loves you!

The name of the LORD *is a strong tower; the righteous run to it and are safe.—Proverbs 18:10*

Chapter 5
Pray and Process

Adoration: Most High, I love you because you are gentle with me. You know how to lead my family, and your timing is always perfect. You made all the nations. You made the universe with all the planets, stars, and galaxies. How marvelous are your works!

Confession: Lord Jesus, I have sinned because I am in fear once again. Forgive me, and fill me with strong faith to follow you wherever you lead me. I repent of not always going to You *first*. I need you to help me change that in my life.

Thanksgiving: Almighty God, we thank you for keeping us safe from robbers and thieves, and for providing our family with everything we need. I am so thankful that you love me and that you are increasing my faith in You.

Supplication: Holy Spirit of the living God, I need your comfort in difficult situations that take place in my life. I pray for missionaries around the globe. Some places are underground, and they need your protection. They need your wisdom and guidance in all that they say or do.

Process What You Have Learned

1. How much of Jesus is in you? A little or all of you? Would you say that the Jesus in you is growing—more of Him and less of you?

2. Applying this chapter to your own life, what circumstances are you facing right now?

3. Do you have fear about these circumstances? What could be the source of that fear?

4. Is God calling you to go forward to serve Him?

CHAPTER 6

The Most High Covers You

He will cover you with his feathers,
and under his wings you will find refuge;
his faithfulness will be your shield and rampart.

—Psalm 91:4

I LOVE THE mind picture I receive from this verse: a cover. I think of a soft, downy quilt that covers me with warmth. I curl up in the folds, and peaceful rest and security surround me. I also think of a bomb shelter in Israel where the children are covered, protected from a barrage of rockets. I think of God overshadowing us—the covering of the Most High.

We see seven key sets of words in verse 4.

HE

1. **HE**: He is the Most High God, El Elyon.

COVERS

2. HE WILL **COVER**: The verb cover means to hedge, fence about, shut in; to block, overshadow; to stop the approach, shut off; to screen, protect; to weave together.

YOU

3. HE WILL COVER **YOU**: You are important to God. He knows all about you. He wants you to know all about Him—His love for you, how He cares for you. He wants to be close to you. Open your heart to these words that we are learning. God has made us all unique. Your mind picture of a cover may be different than mine. I hope that as I share my picture with you on these pages, you will receive your own personal perspective of these verses. This is exactly what happened when I spoke at a women's retreat several years ago. After we learned Psalm 91, we created a quilt. Every square was different, and each one represented a mind-picture revelation that the Holy Spirit gave each person.

Another example of a cover is a bomb shelter. That is quite different from a quilt as an example, isn't it? There are cities in Israel that are constantly under siege from rockets. Thousands of rockets have been fired into Israel in the last fourteen years. This has caused a generation of children to be traumatized by these ongoing attacks. Bomb shelters have been built to protect against this onslaught and to bring these children the protection and care they so desperately need.

HIS FEATHERS—HIS WINGS

4. HE WILL COVER YOU WITH **HIS FEATHERS** AND **UNDER HIS WINGS**: These references speak figuratively of protection and care.

A bird's nest is a perfect example from nature showing how God cares for us. The nest is woven from different things that the birds find. They weave it into a safe refuge for their young. When I teach this verse, I use the nest that was in our flowering tree as a visual. We were delighted to find an active nest right next to our picture window. We checked on it often. Late one night during a thunderstorm, I awoke and went to the window to see if the nest was safe. The wind blew and the tree swayed, but this little nest remained safe. The birds survived the storm. Just like those little birds, we are covered by God and kept safe in the storms of life. Jesus tells us about God's care using the illustration of birds:

Are not two sparrows sold for a penny? Yet not one of them will fall to the ground outside your Father's care. And even the very hairs of your head are all numbered. So don't be afraid; you are worth more than many sparrows.—Matthew 10:29–31

There are other verses that speak of God's wings.

Keep me as the apple of your eye; hide me in the shadow of your wings.—Psalm 17:8

How priceless is your unfailing love, O God! People take refuge in the shadow of your wings.—Psalm 36:7

Have mercy on me, my God, have mercy on me, for in you I take refuge. I will take refuge in the shadow of your wings until the disaster has passed.—Psalm 57:1

I long to dwell in your tent forever and take refuge in the shelter of your wings.—Psalm 61:4

Because you are my help, I sing in the shadow of your wings.—Psalm 63:7

You are my hiding place; you will protect me from trouble and surround me with songs of deliverance.—Psalm 32:7

You are my hiding place and my shield: I hope in thy word.—Psalm 119:114 (KJV)

REFUGE
5. HE WILL COVER YOU WITH HIS FEATHERS AND UNDER HIS WINGS YOU WILL FIND **REFUGE**: Refuge is a shelter.

We looked at refuge in verse 2. Psalm 91 mentions the word "refuge" three times. We will see it a third time in verse 9. We can be sure that Moses valued the Most High, his refuge, because Moses saw God deliver him time after time. He knew God was covering him.

FAITHFULNESS/TRUTH

6. HE WILL COVER YOU WITH HIS FEATHERS AND UNDER HIS WINGS YOU WILL FIND REFUGE; **HIS FAITHFULNESS**: The NIV uses the word faithfulness, and the NJKV uses the word truth. Look closely at this definition from the Hebrew word *'emeth*, which means truth: (1) firmness, faithfulness; truth: (a) sureness, reliability;

His faithfulness shall be thy shield and buckler.
His truth will be your shield and buckler. (NKJV)

When we make God our refuge, God also shows us His truth. One day I was driving in the car, and I was confused about which church to attend. Geographically, I was between two churches that were about five miles apart. I cried out to the Lord, "Which church should I attend, this one or that one? I don't know the way. What's the way, Lord?" The Lord spoke to my heart immediately. He said, "I am the way." My confusion left, and my mind was at peace. He will guide you with His words.

Jesus answered, "I am the way and the truth and the life. No one comes to the Father except through me."—John 14:6

O, send out your light and your truth! Let them lead me. Let them lead me to your holy hill and to your tabernacle.—Psalm 43:3 (NKJV)

[Even] the Spirit of truth. *The world cannot accept him, because it neither sees him nor knows him. But you know him, for he lives with you and will be in you.—John 14:17*

When the Advocate comes, whom I will send to you from the Father—the Spirit of truth *who goes out from the Father—he will testify about me.—John 15:26*

But when he, the Spirit of truth, *comes, he will guide you into all truth. He will not speak on his own; he will speak only what he hears, and he will tell you what is yet to come.—John 16:13*

When we read the story of Moses leading the children of Israel out of Egypt, we see the faithfulness of God.

SHIELD AND RAMPART/BUCKLER

7. HE WILL COVER YOU WITH HIS FEATHERS, AND UNDER HIS WINGS YOU WILL FIND REFUGE; HIS FAITHFULNESS WILL BE YOUR **SHIELD AND RAMPART**: The shield and rampart are pieces of armor that protected the body, especially the vital organs, from the enemy's weapon thrusts and arrows.

The first four verses of this psalm are full of symbols so that we may understand how great our God is and how important the truth is. These symbols help us realize God's power in our lives. Moses was telling the people that God is mighty and is very willing to protect them from the enemy who comes to destroy them.

Chapter 6
Pray and Process

Adoration: Most High, I love you because I have seen your hand on my life. You have been a shield to me. You have been faithful to me. You have given me truth. I have seen you be my refuge.

Confession: Lord Jesus, I sinned when I doubted you or refused to see the truth. Forgive me. I don't want to doubt you anymore. Give me truth in my inmost parts. I sinned when I chose not to go your way. Teach me your way.

Thanksgiving: Almighty God, I thank you for saving me and showing me how to live in your ways. Thank you for pulling me out of my pit. Thank you for your hand on my life. You rescued me even when I didn't deserve it. Thank you. I am coming back to thank you!

Supplication: Holy Spirit of the living God, I pray that all my family and friends and coworkers will find you. I pray that you will change all of our lives. We need you to help us every day. We want you to come into our lives and give us truth more and more.

Process What You Have Learned

1. When has the Lord covered you and averted a tragedy in your life?

2. What is your mind picture when I speak of a cover?

3. Tell a time when God showed you His faithfulness and truth.

4. Do you get a mind picture of a shield or buckler that applies to your life?

Fear? No More Fear!

You will not fear the terror of night,
nor the arrow that flies by day,
nor the pestilence that stalks in the darkness, nor the
plague that destroys at midday. A thousand may fall
at your side, ten thousand at your right hand,
but it will not come near you.
You will only observe with your eyes and
see the punishment of the wicked.

—PSALM 91:5–8

IN THE NKJV, we read, "You shall not be afraid." There is a command in this verse to not fear. Imagine the scene here. Moses is leading millions of people out of Egypt. Pharaoh finally said that they could go. The Israelites realize that Pharaoh has changed his mind and is coming after them with his army. They are in the desert with nowhere to go, Pharaoh and the army are behind them, and the Red Sea is before them. They are trapped! But Moses is telling them everything is going to be all right and to trust the Most High.

We observe seven key points in these verses.

FEAR

1. YOU WILL NOT **FEAR**: *Yare'* in Hebrew means fear, revere, be afraid. The Israelites were coming out of Egypt into the wilderness. There was a lot to be

afraid of especially when they saw Pharaoh and his army coming after them. The Bible talks a lot about fear. We know that God commands us not to be afraid. Fear is the opposite of faith.

TERROR OF NIGHT

2. YOU WILL NOT FEAR THE **TERROR OF NIGHT:** *Pachad* in Hebrew means terror or dread. This can mean the enemy coming who terrifies us; fears in us just because it's dark; wild animals in the wilderness, bombs, thunderstorms.

ARROW THAT FLIES BY DAY

3. YOU WILL NOT FEAR THE TERROR OF NIGHT NOR **THE ARROW THAT FLIES BY DAY**: Chets in Hebrew means arrows, archers, thunderbolts. These are the arrows of the enemy. Today's application might be the rockets fired at Israel every day. They can actually see the rockets coming in the daytime. Iran has threatened to wipe Israel off the map. These are all the things that bring fear to our souls.

PESTILENCE/ PLAGUE

4.. YOU WILL NOT FEAR THE TERROR OF NIGHT NOR THE ARROW THAT FLIES BY DAY, NOR THE **PESTILENCE THAT STALKS IN THE DARKNESS:** *Deber* in Hebrew means pestilence or plague. We saw this same word defined in Chapter 4. The pestilence refers to the plagues in Egypt. Currently this refers to diseases coming on the earth—viruses like Ebola, HIV, diseases that result from natural disasters like cholera, and malaria and other epidemics.

PLAGUE THAT DESTROYS AT MIDDAY

5. YOU WILL NOT FEAR THE TERROR OF NIGHT NOR THE ARROW THAT FLIES BY DAY, NOR THE PESTILENCE THAT STALKS IN THE DARKNESS, **NOR THE PLAGUE THAT DESTROYS AT MIDDAY**: This is a metaphor for dangers that come by day. Currently this would include earthquakes, tsunamis, tornadoes, famines, floods, and disease.

A THOUSAND/TEN THOUSAND

6. A THOUSAND MAY FALL AT YOUR SIDE, TEN THOUSAND AT YOUR RIGHT HAND, BUT IT WILL NOT COME NEAR YOU: What could this mean in our world today? A thousand rockets; ten thousand missiles; a thousand bullets—ten thousand grenades; an army of a thousand or ten thousand?

SEE

7. YOU WILL ONLY OBSERVE WITH YOUR EYES AND **SEE** THE PUNISHMENT OF THE WICKED. Using the illustration of the Israelites, the plagues that they saw in Egypt; the Egyptian army and all their chariots were about to be destroyed by the waters of the Red Sea and the Israelites were going to *see* God defend them when they were defenseless.

At the beginning of Exodus 14, we read that the Lord is revealing the future to Moses. As the story continues, we see that the people do not know the ways of God. God gave a leader, Moses, to teach the people. God's way is revealed here: "It is not going to come near you." How did Moses know the ways of God? Moses had his ears tuned to God's voice. The Most High is going to save His people from destruction by the approaching Egyptian army. We have to listen to God to learn His ways.

"For my thoughts are not your thoughts, neither are your ways my ways," declares the Lord. "As the heavens are higher than the earth, so are my ways higher than your ways and my thoughts than your thoughts. As the rain and the snow come down from heaven, and do not return to it without watering the earth and making it bud and flourish, so that it yields seed for the sower and bread for the eater, so is my word that goes out from my mouth: It will not return to me empty, but will accomplish what I desire and achieve the purpose for which I sent it."—Isaiah 55:8–11

The word of the Lord to Moses is: I am going to save my people. But the Israelites complain:

As Pharaoh approached, the Israelites looked up, and there were the Egyptians, marching after them. They were terrified and cried out to the LORD. They said to

Moses, "Was it because there were no graves in Egypt that you brought us to the desert to die? What have you done to us by bringing us out of Egypt? Didn't we say to you in Egypt, 'Leave us alone; let us serve the Egyptians'? It would have been better for us to serve the Egyptians than to die in the desert!"—Exodus 14:10–12

Fear causes people to complain. I can understand that they were terrified when they saw the Egyptians. I can admit that I would have been terrified too. This was the unexpected. The last thing they ever expected was that Pharaoh would change his mind and come after them. They had been through so much! We see a lesson for our own lives again. We start going to church. We read our Bibles. We pray. We begin to walk in the freedom that God has given us. Good things are happening. We feel the joy. Then the enemy comes after us. He tries to steal, kill, and destroy in our lives. We don't expect any trouble, but trouble shows up. There it is. We become fearful, and we begin to complain: "It would have been better if I hadn't read my Bible. It would have been better if I hadn't gone to church. It would have been better if I hadn't prayed." At this point, we are in unbelief. The enemy of our souls has planted seeds of doubt because he doesn't want to lose us to the Kingdom of God. This is what the result is: we don't trust God. We begin to complain against God. But believers do not fear or complain. They know that God will rescue them. The Bible tells us that nothing is impossible with God.

Moses knew God had a plan because He knew God. We are learning to know God. We have to say "no" to the enemy and tell God we believe and trust in Him.

Look closely at your life. Are you complaining or do you trust God to deliver you! Let's read on!

> *And Moses answered the people, "Do not be afraid. Stand firm and you will see the deliverance the Lord will bring you today. The Egyptians you see today you will never see again. The Lord will fight for you; you need only to be still.—Exodus 14:13–14*

Moses was telling them important points that apply to our lives today.

- Do not be afraid.
- Stand firm.
- *See* the deliverance the Lord will bring you.
- The Lord will fight for you—be still.

Let's look at the definition of faith to understand how we are to live.

> *Faith is the confidence in what we hope for and assurance about what we do not see.—Hebrews11:1*

> *For we live by faith, not by sight.—2 Corinthians 5:7*

But the Israelites were in unbelief. Believers don't complain. We too must learn that we have to trust God again and again. This is a continual believing that God has a plan for our lives. We continue to believe that God will help us in our circumstances. We learn what it means to stand firm with faith. We learn to see with eyes of faith when we find ourselves in unexpected circumstances.

> *And Moses stretched out his hand over the sea; and the Lord caused the sea to go back by a strong east wind all that night, and made the sea dry land and the waters*

were divided. And the Lord said, "Stretch forth your hand..." And the waters returned and covered the chariots, and the horsemen, and all the host of Pharaoh that came into the sea after them; there remained not so much as one of them. And Israel saw that great work which the Lord did upon the Egyptians.—Exodus 14:21–31

This brings us back to Psalm 91:8:

A thousand may fall at your side, ten thousand at your right hand, but it will not come near you. You will only observe with your eyes and see the punishment of the wicked.

These verses from the Book of Exodus help us understand why we cannot murmur or complain. Apply this story to your life and ask yourself, "What does my faith say?"

So faith comes from hearing, that is, hearing the Good News about Christ.— Romans 10:17. NLT

- My faith says: I do not have to fear the terror of night (v. 5).
- My faith says: I do not have to fear arrows in the day (v. 5).
- My faith says: I do not have to fear pestilences (v. 6).
- My faith says: I do not have to fear noonday destructions (v. 6).
- My faith says:the destroyer does not come near me (v. 7).
- My faith is a GIFT from God.

For it is by grace you have been saved, through faith—and this is not from yourselves, it is the gift of God.—not by works, so that no one can boast. Ephesians 2:8

God moved mightily and rescued them. We see later in the story when the Israelites are in the wilderness how much God dislikes complaining. We don't want to be found speaking against God. He has to deal harshly with the Israelites because of their unbelief. We will see this in Chapter 9 on pages 77-78.

Now the people complained about their hardships in the hearing of the Lord, and when he heard them his anger was aroused. Then fire from the Lord burned among them and consumed some of the outskirts of the camp.—Numbers 11:1

But the people grew impatient on the way; they spoke against God and against Moses, and said, "Why have you brought us up out of Egypt to die in the wilderness? There is no bread! There is no water! And we detest this miserable food!"And the Lord sent venomous snakes among them; they bit the people and many Israelites died.—Numbers 21:4-6

And they say, "How does God know? And is there knowledge in the Most High?"—Psalm 73:11

Chapter 7
Pray and Process

Fill in the spaces with your own adoration, confession, thanksgiving, and prayer and supplication.

Adoration: Most High, I love you because...

Confession: Lord Jesus, I have failed to live...

Thanksgiving: Almighty God, I thank you for...

Supplication: Holy Spirit of the living God, I...

Process What You Have Learned

1. Is complaining a reality in your life? What do you fear? Sometimes making a list helps us come to grips with our fears, and we hear our complaints.

2. Do you complain and murmur about the people in your life because they have so many faults?

3. When did you lose trust in God? If you allow the Holy Spirit to show you, your trust in God can be restored. He cares about you.

4. If you are complaining about something, is it because you don't believe that God can bring change to your situation?

CHAPTER 8

Deciding to Live with the Most High

If you say, "The Lord is my refuge," and you make
the *Most High* your *dwelling,* no *harm will overtake
you,* no *disaster will come near* your tent.

—PSALM 91:9–10

MOSES CONTINUES TO speak to the people in these verses. He is telling the Israelites that the blessings of God depend on how they respond to God. We find five important sets of words in these verses that need to be defined.

IF

1. **IF**: Moses is speaking directly to the people. He has been teaching them the Lord's ways. He has been telling them that God will cover them. He will be a refuge and He will be faithful. Moses has told them not to fear anything. Now he instructs them how to receive these blessings from God.

YOU SAY

2. IF **YOU SAY:** the emphasis is on the word *You.* Moses can encourage, in-spire, and teach the people but it is up to each individual to commit themselves to the Lord and believe that God has made Moses a leader they must follow. The verb *say* is to speak with the mouth. In Chapter 3, we established that it is

very important to speak right things. Moses expressed his heart change when he exclaimed: *The Lord is my refuge, my fortress, my God, in Him will I trust.* What we say is connected to our hearts. The proof of a heart change expresses itself in the tongue.

> *The mouth of the righteous is a fountain of life, but the mouth of the wicked conceals violence. Proverbs 10:11*

The Pharisees, who were the religious leaders of the time, accused Jesus's disciples of being defiled because they broke tradition and did not wash their hands before they ate. This is what Jesus had to say to them:

> *"You hypocrites! Isaiah was right when he prophesied about you:*
> *'These people honor me with their lips, but their hearts are far from me. They worship me in vain; their teachings are merely human rules.'"* (Isaiah 29:13)

> *Jesus called the crowd to him and said, What goes into someone's mouth does not defile them, but what comes out of their mouth, that is what defiles them. Matthew 15:7-11*

THE LORD IS MY REFUGE

3. IF YOU SAY **"THE LORD IS MY REFUGE":** In verse 9, Moses is asking if the Israelites can *say* that the Lord is their refuge. Moses is encouraging a heart change in his people.

YOU MAKE THE MOST HIGH YOUR DWELLING

4. IF YOU SAY "THE LORD IS MY REFUGE" AND **YOU MAKE THE MOST HIGH YOUR DWELLING:** *Make (in Hebrew suwm)* is the verb that means to put, set, lay, appoint, give, consider. This is a decision for the individual. Even not taking action on something in your life is a decision. *You say* and *you make.*

NO HARM, NO DISASTER

5. IF YOU SAY "THE LORD IS MY REFUGE" AND YOU MAKE THE MOST HIGH YOUR DWELLING **NO HARM SHALL OVERTAKE YOU, NO DISASTER WILL COME NEAR YOUR TENT.:** Moses is telling the people that their protection depends on them dwelling or living with the Most High. He promises that the Most High can be their refuge because (or if) they have responded to the Lord's invitation. This is a promise from the Lord.

You have chosen to live with and abide in the Lord, the Most High. Because of this decision, you receive a promise: *no harm will befall you, no disaster will come near your tent.* There is a reward for yielding to God! He is not a far-off God that we cannot reach.

As we continue on our journey from verse 1 to 10, we see a forward momentum.

- We are learning God's names and God's ways.
- We are memorizing the verses.
- We are making decisions for our lives that include the Most High.
- We are drawing closer to God.
- We are receiving truth about God.

Sometimes, when bad things happen to us, we get disappointed and say, "The Word of God didn't work for me." But God is not done working in your life. Remember, when Moses stood and faced Pharaoh things got worse. Yet God had a plan to set all the Israelites free from slavery. God's plan would take time to unfold. Believe the Most High so that He can unfold the plan for your life. Believe it in your heart and say it with your mouth.

> *"For I know the plans I have for you," declares the LORD, "plans to prosper you and not to harm you, plans to give you hope and a future. Then you will call on me and come and pray to me, and I will listen to you. You will seek me and find me when you seek me with all your heart." Jeremiah 29:11-13*

I discovered a preacher from the Nineteenth Century who explained these verses so well and gave an example from his own experience. I cannot improve on what he taught me. His name is Charles H. Spurgeon (1834-1892) and he was England's best-known preacher for most of the second half of the nineteenth century. In *The Treasury of David* Volume 2, he expounds on the words *refuge* and *dwelling* found in Psalm 91.

"He who makes God his refuge shall find him a refuge; he who dwells in God shall find his dwelling protected. We must make the Lord our habitation by choosing him for our trust and rest, and then we shall receive immunity from harm; no evil shall touch us personally, and no stroke of judgment shall assail our household.

The dwelling here intended by the original was only a tent, yet the frail covering would prove to be a sufficient shelter from harm of all sorts. It matters little whether our abode be a gypsy's hut or a monarch's palace if the soul has made the Most High its habitation. Get into God and you dwell in all good, and ill is banished far away. It is not because we are perfect or highly esteemed among men that we can hope for shelter in the day of evil, but because our refuge is the Eternal God, and our faith has learned to hide beneath his sheltering wing.

Spurgeon further explains with great conviction why evil cannot touch the people of God.

It is impossible that any ill should happen to the man who is beloved of the Lord; the most crushing calamities can only shorten his journey and hasten him to his reward. Ill to him is no ill, but only good in a mysterious form. Losses enrich him, sickness is his medicine, reproach is his honour, death is his gain. No evil in the strict sense of the word can happen to him, for everything is overruled for good. Happy is he who is in such a case. He is secure where others are in peril, he lives where others die.

Personal Story of God's Protection 1854

How timeless God's Word is! Charles Spurgeon, in 1854, just four years after his conversion, then only twenty, became pastor of London's famed New Park Street Church. This is a story he relates before preaching on Psalm 91.

London's famed New York Park Street Church

He [Spurgeon] gives this personal testimony before his commentary on Psalm 91:9-10 in *The Treasury of David*, Volume 2, page 92.

Before expounding these verses I cannot refrain from recording a personal incident illustrating their power to soothe the heart, when they are applied by the Holy Spirit. In London twelve months, the neighborhood in which I laboured was visited by Asiatic cholera, and my congregation suffered from its inroads.

Family after family summoned me to the bedside of the smitten, and almost every day I was called to visit the grave. I gave myself up with youthful ardour to the visitation of the sick, and was sent for from all corners of the district by persons of all ranks and religions. I became weary in body and sick at heart. My friends seemed falling one by one, and I felt or fancied that I was sickening like those around me.

A little more work and weeping would have laid me low among the rest; I felt that my burden was heavier than I could bear, and I was ready to sink under it. As God would have it, I was returning mournfully home from a funeral, when my curiosity led me to read a paper which was wafered up in a shoemaker's window in the Dover Road.

It did not look like a trade announcement, nor was it, for it bore good bold handwriting these words:

> *Because thou hast made the Lord,*
> *which is my refuge,*
> *even the most High,*
> *thy habitation;*
> *there shall no evil befall thee,*
> *neither shall any plague*
> *come nigh thy dwelling."*
> *Psalm 91:9-10 KJV*

The effect upon my heart was immediate. Faith appropriated the passage as her own. I felt secure, refreshed, girt with immortality. I went on with my visitation of the dying in a calm and peaceful spirit; I felt no fear of evil, and I suffered no harm. The providence which moved the tradesman to place those verses in his window I gratefully acknowledge, and in the remembrance of its marvelous power I adore the Lord my God.

Rhema Words

Here, we need a simple explanation for a not so simple subject: the Greek words *logos* and *rhema*. *Logos* refers to the written Word of God and *rhema* is the uttered Word of God. My goal is to give you examples of rhema words so that you can begin to experience this for yourself. You need to know that this is available to all believers.

Charles Spurgeon experienced what we call a *rhema* word. When the Holy Spirit reveals the Word of God to us personally, we know, without a shadow of a doubt, that God is speaking that Word to us for our present situation. Charles Spurgeon read this verse in a store window, and the words became life and pierced his inner being. He said, "Faith appropriated the passage as her own." Charles knew God was speaking to him and he received the Word into his being. What did he receive? He *felt secure, refreshed, girt with immortality… continued his work in a calm and peaceful spirit; he felt no fear of evil, and he suffered no harm.*

We learn and grow from reading the Word (logos) every day. We hear the Word of God preached and proclaimed. This is considered our spiritual food. Just as our bodies need food to live, our soul needs to have the Word of God. Hearing the Word of God increases our faith.

I have had the experience of receiving a *rhema* word from God. The first experience I had was when I was a new Christian reading through the Bible in the Book of Joshua. (I was feeding on the *logos*)

This book of the law shall not depart out of thy mouth; but thou shalt meditate therein day and night, that thou mayest observe to do according to all that is written therein: for then thou shalt make thy way prosperous, and then thou shalt have good success. Have not I commanded thee? Be strong and of a good courage;

be not afraid, neither be thou dismayed: for the Lord thy God is with thee whithersoever thou goest.—Joshua 1:8-9 (KJV)

These verses jumped off the page and into my heart. God was telling me to read the Word every day and to do what it said! I had never had this experience before, and I was amazed that God would speak to me. Then, as I continued to read verse 9, God was telling me not to be afraid and that He was with me! What an awesome day when we hear God speak to us from His Word! It may not be audible; at least, it wasn't for me. But I believe that it was audible for Moses when God called his name.

God speaks to our hearts. Because I have had this experience, I am confident that you can hear God speak to you too. Why am I so confident? We are told in the Bible that God is the same yesterday, today, and forever. It also tells us that God is not a respecter of persons. This basically means that if He did it for me, He will do it for you.

Then it happened again. I was reading the Book of Isaiah. I came to the following verse, and it changed me forever.

And all thy children shall be taught of the Lord; and great shall be the peace of thy children.—Isaiah 54:13 (KJV)

I received this by faith into my heart as a personal promise from God for my children. I have been praying it ever since. I prayed it hundreds of times when they were growing up. Our children go through trials too. These are life lessons of varying degrees—disagreements with friends, physical fights, bullying, anger, and rebellion. So I would pray, "Lord, you said all my children. This one is having issues, Jesus. Don't forget my sons as they struggle with school. Give this daughter peace and teach her your ways. You promised, Lord." This is not being demanding of God. Faith believes what Most High utters to our hearts.

Years later, I have adult children with families of their own, and I am still praying this promise. This verse is a promise for my children and my grandchildren, for children that I have taught in classrooms over the years, and for women that I have mentored. What a wonderful promise from God to soothe our hearts, knowing that the Lord Himself will teach our children and they will have great peace! You too can take hold of this promise for your family.

Rhema words are so uplifting and encouraging. Just think, you have heard an utterance from the Most High! Sometimes we wait many seasons, and then, in God's timing, God speaks to us. During our trial we live according to all that God has taught us. We stand in faith. We continue to pray. We stay in the Word of God. We keep obeying the last thing that God said to us.

I went through a trial that lasted beyond what I thought I could endure. I was tempted to quit what I was doing. By His grace, I did not quit, but I stood in faith, waiting for God's intervention. The day came when the Lord gave me this *rhema* word:

And the God of all grace, who has called you to his eternal glory in Christ Jesus, after you have suffered a little while, He Himself will restore you and make you strong, and firm, and steadfast."—1 Peter 5:10

That day, I took each phrase and savored it and I was comforted knowing that God knew my situation.

"God of all grace"—I know the God of all grace!

"Called"—I am called of God!

"Eternal glory in Christ Jesus"—that's His eternal salvation for me!

"Suffered a little while"—yes, Lord, this has been hurting me, and you know all about it. I don't know how long a *little while* will be but I know that I can trust you in this.

"He Himself will restore you"—this is so personal; *You* are restoring me, Lord!

"Make you strong, and firm, and steadfast"—oh, Lord, I have felt very weak, and utterly shaken to my core, and I am unsteady. I seem to have lost my confidence. Yes, I need all that restored, Lord!

I entered a time of peace. The trial hadn't gone away, but I knew that God saw me in my misery, and there was grace for me to survive the trial.

I have also had the experience of God's Word being living and active.

> *For the word of God is living and active. Sharper than any double-edged sword, it penetrates even to dividing soul and spirit, joints and marrow; it judges the thoughts and attitudes of the heart.*—*Hebrews 4:12*

I walked into a Christian school classroom and at the head of the classroom was an alphabet. Each letter had a Bible verse attached to it. My eyes went to the letter *W* and the verse was, "What time I am afraid I will trust in thee.—Psalm 56:3." This word immediately went into my heart. It became life to me, and it has been in my memory bank ever since—in an instant! I pray this verse all the time when I feel fear trying to come in to my mind. I have to work through the fear and stand on the Word of God. This is where we can see the Word of God living and active in us. God speaks to us!

Think about all the people in the Bible that heard God speak to them. Think of Joseph, Jesus's earthly father, being led by dreams so that he could take care of Mary and Jesus. Think of John the Baptist hearing God's voice and obeying when Jesus came to him to be baptized. Think of Peter being restored after Jesus was resurrected from the dead.

You can have these experiences too!

I believe that God's word is alive and has power. If the Lord quickens a word to you, take it as your own. It will be filled with hope, grace, and joy and peace for whatever you are experiencing. You will be able to weather the storm because you know that Jesus is in the boat with you!

Chapter 8
Pray and Process

Add your own prayers for chapter 8, and adore, confess, and give thanks to God. Pray for the people in your life who are going through trials and difficult circumstances.

Adoration: Most High, I love you because…

Confession: Lord Jesus, I have sinned…

Thanksgiving: Almighty God, I thank you for…

Supplication: Holy Spirit of the living God, I…

Process What You Have Learned

1. Are things getting worse in your life, like they did for Moses? Describe what you are going through.

2. Do you understand the concept that there are conditions for blessings that we receive from God? Explain it.

3. Have you received a rhema word from God? Write it here.

4. What experiences would you like to ask God to give you?

CHAPTER 9

The Most High Gives Us His Angels

For He will command his angels concerning
you to guard you in all your ways;
They will lift you up in their hands,
so that you will not strike your foot against a stone.
You will tread on the lion and the cobra,
you will trample the great lion and the serpent.

—Psalm 91:11–13

ANGELS COMMANDED

1. FOR HE WILL **COMMAND** HIS **ANGELS CONCERNING YOU:** Tsavah
in Hebrew means to command, charge, give orders, lay charge, give charge to,
order. These are such powerful words that express God's care for us. They declare to us that we are protected by the angels of God. Once again we see God's
goodness. He gives His angels charge over you.

You have probably heard it said that you have a guardian angel that watches
over you. You need to know that there are many angels that guard you when
you have a relationship with the Most High. There are over ninety references to
angels in the Bible. I encourage you to read through these verses. Search and see

what the Bible says about these powerful warrior beings that protect us on the earth. Let's take a look at just a few of the ninety references.

Angels were used by God to announce Jesus's birth and to help Mary and Joseph. God commanded the angels to deliver a message:

> *But the angel said to her: "Do not be afraid, Mary; you have found favor with God. You will conceive and give birth to a son, and you are to call him* Jesus. *He will be great and will be called the* Son of the Most High. *The Lord God will give him the throne of his father David, and he will reign over Jacob's descendants forever; his kingdom will never end."—Luke 1:30–33*

Angels will help with the harvest of souls. When Jesus comes to the earth again in His glory, the angels will be with Him.

I have stated that angels are powerful warrior beings. Here are a few examples that illustrate how mighty angels really are.

- One angel slew 185,000 men in war (2 Chronicles 32:21).
- Peter was chained between two soldiers. Sentries stood guard at the entrance to the prison. Peter's chains fell off his wrists when the angel came to escort him out of the prison (Acts 12:6).
- One angel will seize Satan, bind him, and throw him into the abyss (Rev. 20:1–3).

Following is one of my favorite writings on angels by Charles Spurgeon from *The Treasury of David Volume 2.*

> Not one guardian angel, as some fondly dream, but all the angels are here alluded to. They are the bodyguard of the princes of the blood imperial of heaven, and they have received commission from their Lord and ours to watch carefully over all the interests of the faithful. When men have a charge they become doubly careful, and

therefore the angels are represented as bidden by God himself to see to it that the elect are secured. It is down in the marching orders of the hosts of heaven that they take special note of the people who dwell in God.

GUARD/KEEP

2. FOR HE WILL COMMAND HIS ANGELS CONCERNING YOU **TO GUARD YOU.** Verse 11b: "To keep thee in all thy ways (KJV)": There is a special keeping power that comes from God. He keeps us from evil as He gives His angels charge over us to protect us from the evil one.

> *But the Lord is faithful, and he will strengthen you and protect (keep/guard) you from the evil one.——2 Thessalonians 3:3*

Jesus prays for us:

> *My prayer is not that you take them out of the world but that You protect (keep/guard) them from the evil one.——John 17:15*

God keeps us from the hour of temptation:

> *Because thou hast kept the word of my patience, I also will* keep *thee from the hour of temptation, which shall come upon all the world, to try them that dwell upon the earth.——Revelation 3:10 (KJV)*

> *And the peace of God, which passes all understanding, shall* keep *your hearts and minds through Christ Jesus.——Philippians 4:7*

He keeps us from falling:

> *Now unto him that is able to* keep *you from falling and to present [you] faultless before the presence of his glory with exceeding joy.——Jude 1:24*

I will remain in the world no longer, but they are still in the world, and I am coming to you. Holy Father, protect them by the power of your name, the name you gave me, so that they may be one as we are one.—John 17:11

The angels are commanded by God to keep us in all our ways. We cannot always tell how the angels keep us. Do they repel evil plots against us? Do they keep us from car accidents? Airplane crashes? Disease?

Do not forget to show hospitality to strangers, for by so doing some people have shown hospitality to angels without knowing it.—Hebrews 13:2

You are important to God—He gives His angels charge over you!

Are not all angels ministering spirits sent to serve those who will inherit salvation?—Hebrews 1:14

IN ALL YOUR WAYS.
3. FOR HE WILL COMMAND HIS ANGELS CONCERNING YOU **TO GUARD YOU IN ALL YOUR WAYS.**

Satan tried to use verses 11a and 12 of Psalm 91 when he tempted Jesus. Did you know that the devil can quote the Bible? He deceives by quoting verses falsely. He twists words so that he can fool the ignorant. We need to know what the Word of God says. Satan partially quoted this to Jesus:

"If you are the Son of God," he said, "throw yourself down. For it is written: "He will command his angels concerning you, and they will lift you up in their hands, so that you will not strike your foot against a stone."—Matthew 4:6

Tellingly, Satan left out the phrase "guard [keep] you in all your ways." What a revelation that is! Satan tempts Jesus to throw himself down using the Bible. He misquotes Psalm 91. This revelation clues us in as to how Satan deceives us and misapplies scripture to ensnare us. Satan intentionally stops short of quoting verse 13 because it predicts his own defeat. The lion, cobra, great lion and serpent are all symbols of the enemy. Because of the cross, we can trample the enemy.

> You will tread on the lion and the cobra; you will trample the great lion and the serpent.—Psalm 91:13

Jesus is our example to follow when the devil comes to tempt us. We see that Jesus kept saying, "It is written…"

> Then the devil left him, and angels came and attended him.—Matthew 4:11

Let's look at an example in current times. A man on a motorcycle races down the expressway at 80-100mph. weaving in and out of traffic. He is breaking all the speed limits. Can this man assume that God will give his angels charge over him and protect his reckless ways? That thinking is called presumption. The Oxford English Dictionary gives the meaning as: behavior perceived as arrogant, disrespectful, and transgressing the limits of what is permitted or appropriate. In order for God to protect us, we have to be living in the ways of God. Jesus's reply to Satan after he quoted the Bible:

> It is also written: Do not put the Lord your God to the test.—Matthew 4:7.

When we operate in our own ways, we test God. Jesus stayed in God's ways.

In our continuing story of Moses, we find that time and time again the children of Israel walked in their own ways as they wandered in the wilderness. God told Moses to send some men to explore the land of Canaan. He chose ten men. When they came back, they gave an account to Moses, some of the men said that it was a good land but the people who lived there were too powerful to conquer. Caleb spoke up and recommended that they should go and take possession of the land. He had a good report about the Promised Land. There were eight men who spread a bad report among the people about the land they had explored. The Israelites listened to the bad report and it caused them to grumble against Moses and Aaron. Joshua and Caleb tried to talk to the entire Israelite assembly and convince them that the land was good. They pleaded with them not to rebel against the Lord and not to be afraid.

The people chose to believe the bad report. God told Moses to turn back and set out toward the desert along the route to the Red Sea. Moses spoke to the people everything God had said and told them they were to turn back.

The people rebelled against the Lord and went into the Promised Land without God. They disobeyed the Lord's command.

> *Nevertheless, in their presumption they went up toward the highest point in the hill country, though neither Moses nor the ark of the Lord's covenant moved from the camp. Numbers 14:44*

They presumed that they could do it on their own. They didn't need God. What was the result of their disobedience and grumbling? God said that none of them would go into the Promised Land—only their children would go in. When they went into the land, not heeding Moses's warning to not go, the people of the land came down and attacked them and beat them down all the way to Hormah. God was not with them to protect them. What happened to the men who led this rebellion? Read Numbers 14:36-38. The entire story is found in Numbers 13-14. Don't let Satan tempt you into presumption!

THEY WILL LIFT YOU UP IN THEIR HANDS
4. FOR HE WILL COMMAND HIS ANGELS CONCERNING YOU TO GUARD YOU IN ALL YOUR WAYS; **THEY WILL LIFT YOU UP IN THEIR HANDS SO THAT YOU WILL NOT STRIKE YOUR FOOT AGAINST A STONE:**

Nasa in Hebrew means to lift, bear up, carry, take.
Kaph in Hebrew means the palm, hollow or flat of the hand.

Nagaph in Hebrew means strike, dash, stumble.

The angels are commanded by the Most High to lift us, bear us up, and carry us in their hands and protect our feet from stumbling.

What an awesome God we serve!

TREAD/TRAMPLE—SATAN IS UNDER OUR FEET
5. YOU WILL **TREAD** ON THE LION AND THE COBRA; YOU WILL **TRAMPLE** THE GREAT LION AND THE SERPENT:

Darak in Hebrew means to tread with the feet, to trample.

In verse 13, Moses uses symbols to describe the enemy: lion, cobra, great lion, and the serpent. Every child of God has enemies. They are numerous. They are subtle and powerful, new and old. Yet we will obtain a complete victory over our enemies—"you will tread." When we pray, we put our enemies under our feet. God gives us power and authority to trample them. On the cross, Jesus conquered the enemy. The cross is where we get the power and authority to trample our enemies.

For our struggle is not against flesh and blood, but against the rulers, against the authorities, against the powers of this dark world and against the spiritual forces of evil in the heavenly realms. Ephesians 6:12

Jesus speaks the Word, saying, "It is written." We must know the Word of God to be able to stand against the devil. Here again we see power in the spoken Word. When believers walk in truth and talk in truth, Satan cannot deceive them. We are not ignorant of Satan's devices. He will try to tempt and mislead, prod and taunt, but if you know that Jesus defeated Satan on the cross, you can use the authority that Jesus bought for you and walk in victory. You can tread on Satan and all that he tries to do to you. Sometimes when I pray, I literally stomp my feet because of this verse. I can tread on the enemy and his lies against me and against those whom I love!

Jesus told us that the thief (Satan) comes to steal, kill, and destroy. We can let Satan steal from us, or we can resist him and make him leave us. Jesus came to give us abundant life. The decision is yours. I urge you to live the life of abundance that Jesus bought for you on the cross. Jesus paid the price for you!

Jesus speaks of the angels:

> *"Put your sword back in its place," Jesus said to [Peter], "for all who draw the sword will die by the sword. Do you think I cannot call on my Father, and he will at once put at my disposal more than twelve legions of angels?"—Matthew 26:52–53*

PRAYER IS ONE OF OUR WEAPONS

In Daniel 10, Daniel prays, and there is warfare in the heavens. This is one of the few times that an angel is named—He is called Michael.

> *At that time [the End Times], Michael, the great prince who protects your people, will arise. There will be a time of distress such as has not happened from the beginning of nations until then. But at that time your people—everyone whose name is found written in the book—will be delivered.—Daniel 12:1*

Michael is mentioned again in Revelation:

> *Then war broke out in heaven. Michael and his angels fought against the dragon, and the dragon and his angels fought back.—Revelation 12:7*

In the Book of Acts, a man named Cornelius had a vision of an angel that was sent to him to give him a message about Peter. Peter came to his house and preached. Cornelius had gathered a large number of people, and he and all who were with him were saved and baptized in the Holy Spirit. See Acts 10:1–8 and 10:30.

I mentioned earlier an angel who was sent to release Peter from prison. Look closely at what the church was doing when Peter was in prison:

> *So Peter therefore was kept in prison, but constant prayer was offered to God for him by the church. And when Herod was about to bring him out, that night Peter*

was sleeping, bound with two chains between two soldiers; and the guards before the door were keeping the prison. Now behold, an angel of the Lord stood by him, and a light shone in the prison; and he struck Peter on the side and raised him up, saying, "Arise up quickly!" And his chains fell off his hands.—Acts 12:5–7

"Constant prayer was offered to God"—when we pray, God sends his angels to help us!

Billy Graham, the great evangelist, teaches about Psalm 91 and shares a testimony of angels in his devotional book *Unto the Hills*.

Angels Guard Missionaries in China

If you read and reread this beautiful Psalm, you will discover that in Him we have a permanent abode and residence, and that all of the comfort, security, and affection which the human heart craves is found in Him.

Modern psychiatrists say that one of the basic needs of man is security. In this psalm we are assured that in God we have the greatest of security: "There shall no evil befall thee, neither shall any plague come nigh thy dwelling. For he shall give his angels charge over thee, to keep thee in all thy ways" (Ps. 91:10–11KJV).

A few years ago in China, two Christian missionaries were undergoing bitter persecution. One night as they were getting ready to retire, they heard the sound of voices outside the compound. They lifted the blinds to find their home surrounded with belligerent men who had gathered there to terminate the couple's ministry.

The missionary husband and wife, realizing that God was their only refuge, dropped on their knees and prayed for those who would harm them, and reminded God that He had promised to be with them even unto the end. When they arose from their knees, they noticed that the crowd was dispersing, and the excited murmuring of the departing mob indicated that something unusual had happened. The missionaries thanked God for answered prayer and retired. The next morning as the sun cast its rays upon the compound, a native Christian came to the door and begged an audience with the missionary.

"Do you know why the mob did not kill you last night?" he asked.

"Our God-answered prayer," replied the missionary.

"Yes," said the native man. "When you were on your knees last night, four creatures like angels, dressed in robes of white, appeared, and one stood at each corner of your house. The mob trembled and fled, and we Christians who stood helpless in the crowd knew that once more God had intervened."

Chapter 9
Pray and Process

(Please feel free to add your own words as well.)

Adoration: Most High, we love you because you have given us everything: your Son, angels, your Word, your love. You shed your blood for us. We worship you!

Confession: Lord Jesus, I sometimes forget that you have equipped us with all these things, and I do not use the power that you have given me to bring the Kingdom to those around me. Forgive me.

Thanksgiving: Almighty God, we thank you for the Cross, for your blood that you shed, for your stripes, for your Word, and for our brothers and sisters in Christ.

Supplication: Holy Spirit of the living God, I pray that you would wake us up, that you will sweep over the United States with revival power. We ask you for a mighty outpouring of your Holy Spirit on every tribe, every tongue, and every nation. Let the glory of the Lord cover the earth as the waters cover the seas.

Process What You Have Learned

1. What have you learned about the angels that you didn't know before?

2. Have you ever been tempted? Did you use the Word against the enemy?

3. Can we live any way we want and expect the angels to protect us?

4. Go to www.biblegateway.com and look up all the verses on angels in your favorite Bible translation.

CHAPTER 10

Loving God

"Because he loves me," says the Lord,
"I will rescue him, I will protect him,
for he acknowledges my name."

—PSALM 91:14

THESE WORDS ARE spoken directly by God Himself: "Because he loves me..." God is speaking in the first person, and He is a making a promise. Let's look at the seven key points in this verse.

BECAUSE

1. **BECAUSE**: *Kiy* in Hebrew is translated as because, if, surely.

HE

2. BECAUSE **HE**: This person is the man, teen, woman, or child who is getting close to the Most High.

LOVES

3. BECAUSE HE **LOVES** ME: *Chashaq* in Hebrew means to desire, set his love, delight, in love; to be attached to; long for. The person is desiring, delighting, and in love with the Most High. This relationship is developing into a love affair between God and man. There is a reward for loving God. Moses had that kind of love. I want that kind of love!

LORD

4. BECAUSE HE LOVES ME, SAYS THE **LORD**: Yehovah in Hebrew. Jehovah is "the existing One." We saw this same word in verse two. The title "Lord" expresses honor, dignity, and majesty, and it is used of Jesus as the Messiah in Acts 2:36, Philippians 2:9–11, and Romans 1:4 and 14:8.

RESCUE

5. BECAUSE HE LOVES ME, SAYS THE LORD, I WILL **RESCUE** HIM: *Palat* in Hebrew, means to deliver, (cause to) escape, carry away safe. This verse is the Most High's promise and it declares that He will rescue those who love Him.

PROTECT

6. BECAUSE HE LOVES ME, SAYS THE LORD, I WILL **RESCUE** HIM, I WILL **PROTECT** HIM: In Hebrew *sagab* means to be too high for capture; to be set securely on high. It is important to note that the KJV seems to be a more literal translation and describes God's power to deliver and protect.

Because he has set his love upon me, therefore I will deliver him; I will set him on high, because he has known my name. Psalm 91:14

ACKNOWLEDGES/KNOWS MY NAME

7. BECAUSE HE LOVES ME, SAYS THE LORD, I WILL RESCUE HIM, I WILL PROTECT HIM FOR **HE ACKNOWLEDGES MY NAME**: *Yada* in Hebrew, means to know and to acknowledge. There are three ways to look at the verb to know:

1) To be acquainted with; to discriminate.
2) To know by experience; to recognize.
3) To learn to know; to distinguish.

We have to look at the last part of this verse and ask: What does the person have to know or acknowledge? It's God's name. *Shem* in Hebrew, is used as a designation of God, His name.

We have talked about God's names in previous chapters, and now we see how important it is for us to know and reverence God by each of His names. He wants to reveal His names to us. To paraphrase, God says, "Surely, this one loves me and because he knows and loves my name, I am promising to protect him, rescue him, deliver him and honor him."

It may seem redundant to keep reading the verse word for word as we study each verse separately, but there is a purpose. If you read it over and over, you will easily embed the verse in your memory. Why is it important to memorize Bible verses? We are not sinless, but as we enter into intimacy with God, the desire of our heart is that we want to sin less and less. Holding God's Word in our heart helps keep us from sin.

I have hidden your word in my heart that I might not sin against you.
—Psalm 119:11

Has anyone ever asked you, "Do you love God?" How would you respond to that question? I have heard worship leaders and pastors declare this on behalf of the people present in the church: "We love you, Lord." That's quite a statement. This affirmation resonates with me in my spirit. I agree with the worship leader and the pastor, and with them I declare that I love God. These are Jesus's words:

If you love me, keep my commands.—John 14:15

Jesus said to them, "If God were your Father, you would love me, for I have come here from God. I have not come on my own; God sent me.—John 8:42

[The expert in the law] answered [Jesus], "'Love the Lord your God with all your heart and with all your soul and with all your strength and with all your mind'; and, 'Love your neighbor as yourself.'"—Luke 10:27

As a child, I memorized this prayer, and I believed it:

The Apostle's Creed

I believe in God, the Father Almighty,
Creator of heaven and earth; and
in Jesus Christ, His only Son, our Lord:
who was conceived by the Holy Spirit,
born of the Virgin Mary; suffered
under Pontius Pilate, was crucified, died
and was buried. He descended into hell;
the third day He rose again from the dead;
He ascended into heaven, is seated at the
right hand of God the Father Almighty;
from thence He shall come to judge
the living and the dead. I believe
in the Holy Spirit, the holy catholic church,
the communion of saints, the forgiveness of sins,
the resurrection of the body, and
life everlasting. Amen.

As an adult, I had to commit my life to Jesus. I can know all the above facts in this prayer of my childhood, but do these facts produce the love of God in my heart as I walk as an adult? It isn't a matter of knowing facts. It is a matter of knowing the person, Jesus Christ, who is referred to in this prayer, and believing in Him by faith in my spirit.

> *And without faith it is impossible to please God, because anyone who comes to him must believe that he exists and that he rewards those who earnestly seek Him.*—*Hebrews 11:6*

How can I love a God that I have never seen? Let me tell you about Thomas, one of Jesus's disciples. After Jesus was crucified, died, and rose again, He appeared to his disciples, but Thomas was not with them that day. Here's the account of the story in the Gospel of John:

On the evening of that first day of the week, when the disciples were together, with the doors locked for fear of the Jewish leaders, Jesus came and stood among them and said, "Peace be with you!" After he said this, he showed them his hands and side. The disciples were overjoyed when they saw the Lord. Again Jesus said, "Peace be with you! As the Father has sent me, I am sending you."

Now Thomas (also known as Didymus), one of the Twelve, was not with the disciples when Jesus came. So the other disciples told him, "We have seen the Lord!" But he said to them, "Unless I see the nail marks in his hands and put my finger where the nails were, and put my hand into his side, I will not believe."

A week later his disciples were in the house again, and Thomas was with them. Though the doors were locked, Jesus came and stood among them and said, "Peace be with you!" Then he said to Thomas, "Put your finger here; see my hands. Reach out your hand and put it into my side. Stop doubting and believe." Thomas said to him, "My Lord and my God!" Then Jesus told him, "Because you have seen me, you have believed; blessed are those who have not seen and yet have believed."—John 20:19–20, 24–29

When Jesus said, "Blessed are those who have not seen and yet have believed," He was referring to us! All those who have believed in Jesus for the past two thousand years since the day when Jesus ascended into heaven are referenced in this verse. Jesus prayed for us while He was still on earth.

I pray also for those who will believe in me through their [the disciples'] message, that all of them may be one, Father, just as you are in me and I am in you.—John 17:20b–21

There is a test we can take to determine if we really love God.

Whoever claims to love God yet hates a brother or sister is a liar. For whoever does not love their brother or sister, whom they have seen, cannot love God, whom they have not seen. And he has given us this command: Anyone who loves God must also love their brother and sister.—1 John 4:20–21

Jesus left us a trademark for Christianity, and that trademark is love. He was our example of love. It is the reason we forgive—we love. It is the reason we are not weary in doing good—we love. I mentioned it earlier, but it is worth repeating. Jesus said:

> *By this everyone will know that you are my disciples, if you love one another.*—
> John 13:35

In conclusion, when you say that you love God, it means:

- You believe in His existence—you have concluded this fact in your mind.
- Your belief system has moved from believing facts in your mind to believing by faith in your heart (or spirit).
- You admit that God is higher, stronger, and more intelligent than you.
- You have decided that you need God.
- You are not angry with God.
- You are in relationship with Him.
- You love others.

Jesus says to us: Love the Lord your God with all your heart and soul and mind and strength! We have not seen Jesus with our natural eyes, but we believe in Him!

Chapter 10
Pray and Process

Adoration: Most High, we love you because you first loved us!

Confession: Lord Jesus, I have sinned…I stopped loving and believing in you. Forgive me!

Thanksgiving: Almighty God, we thank you for your mercies that are new every morning. We thank you for the cross. We accept the cross and the forgiveness you offer us.

Prayer: Holy Spirit of the living God, help us to live by faith because we want to please God.

Process What You Have Learned

As we read the Word of God, we are learning to *know* God and see what a loving God He is. Most High sent Jesus to earth for us!

1. Write out 1 John 4:7–8

2. Write out 1 John 4:9–11

3. Write out 1 John 4:16.

4. Write out 1 John 4:18.

CHAPTER 11

Call on the Most High...in Trouble

He will call on me, and I will answer him:
I will be with him in trouble,
I will deliver him, and honor him.

—PSALM 91:15-16

WHAT PROMISES WE have! When Verse 15 talks about calling on God, this refers to prayer. Jesus is our example for prayer. He would be with multitudes of people, and then He would go up on the mountain by Himself to pray. He said that we should go into our room and pray in the secret place (Matt. 6:6). He taught His disciples how to pray what is known as the "Our Father" (Matt. 6:9). There is an Old Testament verse that is very clear about calling upon God. This is God speaking:

If my people, who are called by my name, will humble themselves and pray and seek my face and turn from their wicked ways, then I will hear from heaven, and I will forgive their sin and will heal their land.—2 Chronicles 7:14 (NIV)

In Psalm 91:15–16, the Most High gives us promises to assure us of His great love.

- I can call on the Most High.
- He promises to answer.
- He promises to be with me in trouble.
- He promises that He will deliver me.
- He will honor me. Wow!
- With long life, He will satisfy me.
- He will show me His salvation.

God is telling us that we need to call upon Him. The promise is fulfilled when we humble ourselves and pray. Do you see that prayer comes first? We have set our love on the Most High, on His Son, Jesus Christ, and on the Holy Spirit, our comforter.

> *I have told you these things, so that in me you may have peace. In this world you will have trouble. But take heart! I have overcome the world.—John 16:33*

Jesus told us we would have trouble. Let me ask you: Do you have trouble in your life right now? Do you need a job? Are you facing financial trouble? Is there trouble in your home with a spouse or with your children? Do you have teenagers that are getting into trouble? Jesus said, "Take heart! I have overcome the world." Because Jesus has overcome the world, He can help you overcome whatever is troubling you. We have a RISEN Savior. He loves you!

World Trouble

We have a lot of "trouble" in our world today. There are wars and rumors of wars. Terrorists are attacking people. Hateful people are attacking Israel, her people and the land. Terrorists are beheading Christians. All around the world, people are being martyred for their faith. Anti-Semitism is on the rise once again.

The terrorist behind these attacks is the devil. The devil knows that his time is short. Jesus is coming back soon to rescue Israel and set up His Kingdom on earth for His Millennial Reign. Jesus told us about these things.

I have been taught for years to watch the Middle East. Watch and pray. We are seeing Bible prophecy come to pass. Israel became a nation in 1948. The Jews are God's chosen people, and God has given them the land of Israel. There are nations that want to blow Israel off the map. They refuse to recognize Israel as a nation. I am amazed at this verse in Psalm 83 because it sounds like a current news headline:

> *See how your enemies growl, how your foes rear their heads. With cunning they conspire against your people; they plot against those you cherish. "Come," they say, "let us destroy them as a nation, so that Israel's name is remembered no more."—Psalm 83:2–4*

> *So pursue them with your tempest and terrify them with your storm. Cover their faces with shame, LORD, so that they will seek your name. May they ever be ashamed and dismayed; may they perish in disgrace. Let them know that you, whose name is the LORD—that you alone are the Most High over all the earth.—Psalm 83:15–18*

Family Trouble

On the home scene, we have trouble. Marriages are dissolving, and the family is in jeopardy. God created the family unit. He made Adam and Eve and told them to multiply. They were the first family. He knew that children needed a father and a mother in order to be nurtured and brought up in the ways of the Lord. In all these things, we pray that the Most High will deliver us from trouble in our families.

Political Trouble

Our political systems are in trouble. God's values and ways are not valued by many people. The United States of America was founded on Biblical principles. These principles have helped us to become the nation that we are today.

The terrorist attacks on September 11, 2001, changed the United States forever. We continue to pray that God will protect us in this trouble when other nations attack our way of life and judge us as evil.

To be politically correct is esteemed above doing the right thing or saying the right thing. The Merriam-Webster Dictionary defines political correctness as: conforming to a belief that language and practices which could offend political sensibilities (such as in matters of sex or race) should be eliminated. It has equated into harming religious freedom. As an example, if I choose to pray over my meal in a restaurant this may offend someone. It is said to be politically incorrect and some people want anything religious to stay inside the four walls of a church building. Political correctness can replace my constitutional rights of freedom of speech and freedom of religion. We didn't think we would ever see this kind of trouble in America.

In the United States of America, we have debt that is spiraling out of control. Healthcare costs are mounting. Prescription costs are soaring. We prayerfully ask the Most High to be with us in this trouble and deliver us.

Biblical Trouble

In Moses's life, there was trouble. Hebrews 11 is referred to as the Faith Chapter and explains how Moses's parents dealt with trouble.

> *By faith Moses's parents hid him for three months after he was born, because they saw he was no ordinary child, and they were not afraid of the king's edict.— Hebrews 11:23*

By faith Moses's parents protected him as long as they could, and then they had to trust God with the life of their baby boy. This is faith in action and God always honors faith. Hebrews 11:23 tells us that Moses's parents were not afraid of the laws of the land. The law of the land was that all baby boys were to be killed. We are told the reason for this law in Exodus 1:9–13:

> *"Look," [Pharaoh] said to his people, "the Israelites have become much too numerous for us. Come, we must deal shrewdly with them or they will become even more numerous and, if war breaks out, will join our enemies, fight against us and leave the country." So they put slave masters over them to oppress them with forced labor...but the more they were oppressed, the more they multiplied and spread; so the Egyptians came to dread the Israelites and worked them ruthlessly.*

The faith of Moses's parents saved Moses from being killed. A miracle happened, and baby Moses was protected. Pharaoh's daughter took Moses to live with her. There is more to the miracle: not only did Moses live, but also his own mother nursed him for Pharaoh's daughter!

> *Take this baby and nurse him for me, and I will pay you.*—*Exodus 2:9*

The Bible tells what happened when Moses grew up. He was able to stand before Pharaoh without fear. He took God at His word and kept the Passover just as God had instructed the people to do.

> *By faith Moses, when he had grown up, refused to be known as the son of Pharaoh's daughter. He chose to be mistreated along with the people of God rather than to enjoy the fleeting pleasures of sin. He regarded disgrace for the sake of Christ as of greater value than the treasures of Egypt, because he was looking ahead to his reward. By faith he left Egypt, not fearing the king's anger; he persevered because he saw him who is invisible.*—*Hebrews 11:24–27*

Can we, as Jesus Christ's followers, do what Moses's parents did and have active faith to protect and pray over our children? Can we choose not to be afraid of the laws of our land that are detrimental to our children?

> *By faith he kept the Passover and the application of blood, so that the destroyer of the firstborn would not touch the firstborn of Israel.*—*Hebrews 11:28*

By faith the people passed through the Red Sea as on dry land; but when the Egyptians tried to do so, they were drowned.—Hebrews 11:29

Using Moses as our example helps us decide that we can live by faith too in these troubled times. Do you remember when we began to learn about Moses? He was making excuses to God but because of his relationship with the Most High, Moses's character was changed. Moses learned the ways of God and became God's mighty deliverer—a type of Jesus Christ, the Messiah whom God would send. The Most High changes us as we meet with Him in the secret place.

The following narrative is a true story of a mother who faced tragedy (trouble) in her life. She called on God—He was true to His name—Faithful.

Beloved Sacrifice

Jim's Legacy

It was never clearer how much in awe he was of Jim
Than in his eulogy for him
Where he extolled his accomplishments
As a mentor of young minds
A coach of several sports
Who trained champions and inspired awards
As a businessman and entrepreneur
As a defier of odds
For thirty-seven years
Jim ignored the word can't
And stood taller than any man he knew
Even in his wheelchair
Paralyzed in body
But not in spirit
—Earl Ensroth

The year was 2000. The month was May. I received a call from my sister, Ellen. "Come today. His organs are shutting down." The doctors would be disconnecting all life support this afternoon. They would wait for me to arrive. I started the two-and-a-half-hour drive across Michigan, and my mind whirled. Could he recover? He was young—only fifty-seven. We always knew that one of these infections was going to take his life. He'd been through hundreds of trips to the emergency room since the diving accident that paralyzed him at age twenty. There had been countless bouts with infections. I didn't want to deny the reality, but my heart said, "This can't be it. He wants to live. I just know it…he always wants to live!"

I neared the city. If I stayed on the expressway, I would be at the hospital in ten minutes. I considered going to Mom's house first. She was eighty-six years old. This must be so hard on her. She needed me. Countless thoughts kept swirling in my mind. I decided that I needed to keep on the expressway and proceed to the hospital. I arrived and went straight to the intensive care unit. As I neared Jim's room, I heard the grief-stricken sounds of many young voices. They were members of the track team he coached, crying softly as they surrounded his bed to pray. Could he hear them saying their last good-byes? He was in a coma, but I had heard that people in a coma could hear everything that was going on around them. I found that thought comforting in that moment. If that was true, then he knew how they loved him. He was encircled by their love. They were heartbroken that their coach was slipping from this life. He was such an encouragement to them. Was it possible that he would pull through one more time? The high-school students slowly filed out of the room. I was family, I entered. Dr. Brian was there. He greeted me. No one else was there with us.

Dr. Brian was not only Jim's doctor but also his close friend. Brian had lived with Mom and Jim for a short time when he was in college. Dad died in 1982, so Mom had been a widow for eighteen years. Jim had lived with Mom and Dad since he got out of rehab. When Brian needed a place to stay, Jim told him, "Come live with us. Mom won't mind." Well, Mom was from the generation for whom it wasn't unusual for a family to take a person into their home as a boarder, so that became the arrangement. Brian would pay Mom $6.25 per day for room and board and continue his studies. To me, this is a delightful story. Now here he was, twenty-five years later, a family physician. With a cute grin, Mom would refer to him as her "personal physician." I knew that she was as proud of Brian's accomplishments as if he were her very own flesh and blood. Brian held to the belief that he wouldn't be a doctor today without Jim's encouragement.

Brian made Jim comfortable so that he would not have pain. All the life support machines were removed.

He said to me, "This may take a while. Will you be staying?"

"Yes," I said, "I will be staying."

As I stood at his bedside, my thoughts wandered back to that fateful June day when my brother Jim had his accident. Goodness! It was thirty-seven years ago. The doctors told us he broke his neck and severed his spinal cord. He was in critical condition for the first few days and then he spent a long time in recovery. He went from the hospital to Mary Free Bed Rehab. I have a vivid memory of celebrating with him on his 21st birthday with friends and family when he was in rehab.

What a tragedy! He would never walk again. Mom cried when she looked at his shoes. When Jim had his diving accident, I was just shy of sixteen years old. He had just completed "the best round of golf in his life" with some buddies. Then they ran down the hill to go swimming at Silver Lake. He dove off the end of the dock. You just figure that the water will be deep at the end of the dock, right? Well, it was only two feet deep. The impact immediately broke Jim's neck. He could not move, but he held his breath until his friends turned him over in the water. They thought he was joking around.

When I heard the news, I can remember thinking: Life *is* fragile, isn't it? Wow, a life can be changed in the blink of an eye. Wait! People don't break their necks. That is just a saying: "Get out of that tree before you fall and break your neck." For me, Jim's accident was so mind boggling—this was a permanent injury. I prayed for a miracle day in and day out. The reality became: Jim's life and our family life were changed forever.

My wandering thoughts returned to the hospital room. What was inside of me to be able to endure these heartrending moments? Grace. I had never faced death before, not like this. This was so...up close. There was grace for this and

I could feel it. My thoughts were focused on Jim. I hoped that my love for him was touching him.

Memories came in rapid succession. In the fall season, I was the little sister that adored seeing her big brother play the position of quarterback for our high-school football team. When football ended, Jim played varsity basketball. I loved to see him on the basketball court, and I cheered my heart out. He was so good at sports—what they call a natural. In the spring, he ran track. I was fascinated at how he glided over the hurdles and he was very fast. I was so proud of him and proud to be his little sister!

The thought of releasing Jim's precious life from this temporal earthly place and time into an eternal place and time was very disconcerting. I had control of absolutely nothing in these moments. I knew I had to release Jim—I wasn't supposed to hold onto him. This moment wasn't about me and my desires. I was struggling to let him go into the hands of a loving heavenly Father. The Father knows best. He could heal Jim or take him home. In these moments, faith is everything. You have to believe every day in order to believe in crisis moments. The everyday faith becomes a sure thing. It has served you well time after time. Life happens. You walk out each step of life. Faith has been tested, and you always get to the other side of these hard things. Some circumstances prove harder to take than others. But this faith in a loving God becomes solid like a rock. You can sense it solid underneath you. You trust Him. The grace to face death is strong and firm. You reach for it and it's there coming from God's throne room. Amazing grace is God's unmerited favor. He favors us.

The thoughts of "Is this all there is?" and "There is nothing after this life" were unacceptable, and I chased them out of my mind. I knew that there *was* a purpose to life, a purpose bigger than we could ever imagine. I knew that there was a place without ambulances, hospitals, infections, wheelchairs, and breathing tubes. I knew that there was a place of peace where there was no more death or dying, no sickness, no more crying. No more trouble lurking in darkness.

So long ago now, as Jim recovered from his accident, gradually he became resilient. He began to take his electric wheelchair to watch the kids play football at the church field. One thing led to another and he was able to be involved in what he loved most: sports. The only difference what that now Jim wasn't playing sports—he was coaching.

One of Jim's runners wrote an essay about Jim. It accurately expresses Jim's skillfulness as a coach. Jim framed the essay and hung it on his office wall. It was great encouragement for him.

My Hero
by Kyle Hollern

Many people have a famous hero, but my hero is not famous. He is a man who made a mistake that changed his life forever. His mistake was diving into shallow water. This mistake left him a quadriplegic. Even though he can't use most of his body, he is now a high school track and cross country coach. My hero's name is Jim Gardiner.

There are many great qualities about Mr. Gardiner. One of his greatest qualities is his urge to go on. I don't know if many of us could go on every day without the ability to use our body, but this man can. Another great quality about Mr. Gardiner is he is very caring. He is caring in the way he always does what is right for his athletes, and he does it even though it might not be for the good of the team. These are just two of Mr. Gardiner's many qualities.

Before the accident, Mr. Gardiner played many sports, and he was an all-around great athlete. Now he runs his own business, Ultimate High Sports. He also is known all around the state for pole-vault coaching. Mr. Gardiner is the cross-country and track coach for Grand Rapids Catholic Central High School. Even though he can't participate in sports, he is a great coach. He is not famous, but he is a great person in my life. I believe that everyone can look up to a man like him. It's no wonder then why Jim Gardiner is my hero.

This essay speaks volumes! Coaching pole-vaulting from a wheelchair is totally incredible! Young people need leaders with character. There are thousands of coaches that go unlauded every season. Like the essay says, "They are not famous." They work hard. They are dedicated. They love what they do, and they love the kids they coach. They spend their time. They spend their money. They set an example for the students, who are about to become adults. It is a *beloved sacrifice*. Their lives are full of passion—passion for sports, passion to encourage, passion to challenge young lives to excel. Jim was one of those coaches.

"Confidence was the thing I needed most when I first began to coach," Jim remembered. "I wasn't sure I'd be able to make the kids understand me. I didn't know if sitting in a wheelchair would prevent me from getting across my message. I have that confidence now."

I once asked my mother how she made the decision to take care of Jim.

She said to me, "There wasn't a decision. Dad and I just did it. You do what you have to do."

Life has taught me that everything is a decision. Yes, unexpected things happen in our lives, but we decide how to react to them. Even not taking any action is a decision, and so many lives depend on what we decide to do. Mom and Dad's decision to take care of Jim affected hundreds and hundreds of lives. That's pretty astonishing when you think about it. I observed the daily trouble and admired their conquering spirits. I saw how many people made the decision to come alongside Jim and Mom to help them. All of these people practiced *beloved sacrifice*. It wasn't the easy road for any of those involved.

In all her years of living, Mom had learned that caring for others was important. When there's a need, you meet the need. Mom lived that way all her life. So when Jim said in a newspaper interview that his family was wonderful to him that was only a smidgen of the whole story.

Mom was fifty when Jim had his accident. At the time of his death, she was almost eighty-seven and was still taking care of him. She cooked, washed, and cleaned a two-story colonial with the laundry room in the basement. She was a cook, a nurse, a businesswoman, a scheduler, a payroll administrator, and a dedicated caregiver.

Mom couldn't lift Jim, of course, so wonderful family friends, the MacGregors, bought him a Hoyer lift. This was a precision instrument engineered to get Jim in and out of his wheelchair or bed. Uncle John and Aunt El also provided for a room for Jim to be built on the back of the house. Before that, Jim lived in our dining room. The Catholic Central Boosters Club raised money for a van with a wheelchair lift.

Throughout those thirty-seven years, she scheduled people to come to the house to take care of Jim. There were nurses and orderlies who came to put Jim in bed after they finished their shifts at the hospital. There were so many kindnesses—dinners, desserts, friendships, not to mention all the people who would show up to drive Jim to practice or track meets, or weddings or funerals. There were also people who came to help with the office work for Jim's small business. Friends volunteered their organizational skills. The house on Sylvan Ave S.E. teemed with life. When nurses came, they brought their babies. Mom literally saw these babies grow up in her living room. A lot of growing happens in a thirty-seven-year span of time. So many lives helping…giving… loving…living. Ruth Gardiner entertained and loved these babies while their moms helped bathe and dress Jim for a new day. So many people offering a *beloved sacrifice*. Ruth was an amazing lady, and she made it possible for Jim to coach all those years. Ruth and Jim were a dynamic duo in their own right.

Back in the hospital room, my brain was processing a myriad of memories, standing beside Dr. Brian. Jim lay still before us. Jim had a body, a soul, and a spirit. In these moments, I knew that his body had had enough. That was why his organs were shutting down. His body had endured multiple injuries, multiple infections. His muscles sometimes had horrific spasms that literally threw him out of his bed or his wheelchair. His body got so cold in the winter that it was difficult to warm him up. In the summer, he got so overheated that he asked his friend Steve to pour ice water over his head. Yet he overcame all this trouble in order to coach young people.

As I let him go that day, my struggle ceased and peace flooded my soul. When Jim drew his last breath, he left this earthly place to live in eternity. The Bible tells us: "To be absent from the body is to be present with the Lord." Jim had prayed with one of his caregivers and given his heart to Jesus. He accepted Jesus's beloved sacrifice on the cross, the greatest sacrifice of all. When he did that, he was assured of heaven.

Jim's memory lives on in the hearts of his runners, their parents, his friends, and all who knew of him.

Mom was in the process of building a new home when Jim died. The house was intended to make it easier with the wheelchair. There was a cement ramp inside the garage for easy entry into the house. No more slippery, snowy covered ramps. They planned his bedroom with a shower that was designed for a wheelchair. He would also have a living room and there was a covered porch in the back yard. He was so excited that he would have a place to store the inventory for his business, Ultimate High Sports.

He died in May and Mom moved to the new house in August. It's strange how life gives us bittersweet moments. Mom's move to the new house was wonderful and exciting, and at the same time sad because Jim wouldn't get to enjoy it with her.

Mom lived fifteen more years after Jim died way past 100 years. Five years after Jim died, in August of 2005, she buried her second son, Dan who gallantly fought a cancer battle. That same week Dan died, Jim was awarded the Warren Reynolds Lifetime Achievement Award and was inducted into the Grand Rapids Sports Hall of Fame at a dinner downtown. Mom was there. She was very proud of that award. What an honor after all those years! These were bittersweet moments again. Trouble and honor all in the same week.

Mom was so gracious and strong. I knew that her faith in the Lord was sustaining her once again. We went to her house after the Hall of Fame dinner. All of us sat in a circle. I remember that it was my youngest daughter's golden birthday, twenty five on the twenty-fifth of August. My brother's widow, Margie, was on my right hand and my daughter, Elizabeth was on my left. I had a cake for Elizabeth but how do you transition from death on the one hand and celebrate life on the other hand? I was fixed and couldn't move. I could hardly speak being overwhelmed with grief.

Life went on and Mom missed her sons. She was the oldest of five girls and all of them had passed away before her. Life did become good again. The family would come for visits and she resumed her reading. Some of the runners stayed in touch with Mom and she loved that. She was invited to weddings and showers. She accepted the invitation quite often and enjoyed every minute of the celebrations.

Mom especially loved the Christmas cards everyone would send with pictures of all the new babies and growing families of the track enthusiasts. Mom made photo albums with the pictures she received along with the letters and invitations. She loved notes and letters more than phone calls because she could read them over and over. I would catch a glimpse of her in her office gluing all the memorabilia into the books. She would have a contented smile on her face. She was reliving happy moments.

People were her life—so many lives had touched her life because of Jim! And then there was Steve Johnson. Steve would go golfing with Jim when he visited. Usually Steve was off gallivanting around the world somewhere. After Jim died, Steve would come and visit his cousin and stop in to see Mom. He would bring her the *Wall Street Journal*. Then, after a day or two, Steve would visit again. He and Mom would talk about all the articles of interest. She loved it! He would send flowers on Mom's birthday and at Christmas. She was proud of Steve and created an album for him, too. Steve was just like one of her sons.

Jim's legacy has continued. On August 20, 2016, sixteen years after his death, Catholic Central High School dedicated their new sports complex and named one section Jim Gardiner Track and Field. Jim saw this while it was in the planning stages and when some portions of it were already completed. He knew the men who planned this complex and who chose to put his name on the field. These men wanted the new generation of students to know that Coach Jim Gardiner possessed the qualities of commitment and perseverance. These men knew that Jim encouraged accountability in young people for what they said and did in sports and in daily life. They honored Jim's life of endurance in trouble. As a family, we are blessed that this honor was bestowed on Jim.

Mom's legacy lives on in her family too: caring, giving, loving, living. She kept a journal and called her little notes: "Mementos." I found a tiny treasure as I was going through Mom's notes and journals. This entry was written on June 18, 2000, five weeks after my brother Jim died:

"Thirty-seven years ago today Jim got hurt. I miss you, Jim.——Mom."

Let love and faithfulness never leave you; bind them around your neck, write them on the tablet of your heart. Then you will win favor and a good name in the sight of God and man.——Proverbs 3:3

A life well lived creates an indelible mark on the tablet of the heart. Jim lived well...Mom lived well. Many hearts became sorrowful on that day in May 2000 when they heard that Jim died. The same was true of Mom when she died on August 4, 2015. We celebrate their conquering spirits!

God is our refuge and strength, an ever present help in trouble. Therefore we will not fear though the earth give way and the mountains fall into the heart of the sea, though its waters roar and foam and the mountains quake with their surging. Psalm 46:1-2.

Chapter 11
Prayer and Process

Write your personal prayers of adoration, confession, thanksgiving, and supplication from what is in your heart after reading this chapter.

Adoration: Most High, I love you because…

Confession: Lord Jesus, I am sorry for…please forgive me. I repent of my sins and choose to change my thoughts to line up with your truth.

Thanksgiving: Almighty God, I thank you for…

Supplication: Holy Spirit of the living God…

Process What You Have Learned

1. What trouble is in your life right now?

2. Name a time of your life when you thought you would never make it through.

3. As you read the essay entitled "My Hero," did you think of a person or persons who have made a difference in your life?

4. As you read the essay entitled *Beloved Sacrifice* did it trigger thoughts in your mind of a beloved person in your life?

CHAPTER 12

Long Life

With long life will I satisfy him,
and show him my salvation.

—PSALM 91:16

MOSES LIVED 120 years. He had a long life. Verse 16 concludes the entire psalm with another promise and more encouragement for us. To the person who lives in the secret place of the Most High, to the person who loves God, to the person who speaks faith, to the person who worships, God promises long life and salvation.

We do need to make a note here. I would urge you to reflect on this truth: God is sovereign. Sometimes we see a person who is full of faith and love, and they die suddenly at a young age. We do not see the purpose of that, but I assure you that God has a purpose. We don't know how many days we have on this earth. As you walk with God, you will not understand all things. Troubling times come, and we trust that the sovereign God Most High rules in the affairs of men.

Keep in mind Enoch in the Book of Genesis:

Enoch walked faithfully with God; then he was no more, because God took him away.—Genesis 5:24

Then we have the example of the Israelites who came out of Egypt. They disobeyed and rebelled against God and they all died in the wilderness, except for Joshua and Caleb, who lived long lives.

Can you imagine the disappointment of Joshua and Caleb when Israel didn't go into the Promised Land and they all had to keep wandering in the wilderness? Even though, they saw the Promised Land and walked on it, Joshua and Caleb didn't murmur or complain at this turn of events. They waited for God's promises. At the end of the wandering, after forty long years, when all the adults had died, God told all their children to go enter into the Promised Land, and Joshua led them.

There are so many lessons for us in this story.

- Fear will always get in the way of victory. We must overcome fear.
- Trusting God is the best choice. Our confidence has to be in God.
- Waiting on God will always bring us into God's promises.
- When we murmur or complain, we display an ungrateful heart.
- We need to know what God is saying and obey what He speaks to us.
- God blesses every season of our lives.
- God's blessing is long life.

Are you living in the blessing or are you in the wilderness? Have you ever had a great disappointment? Are you going through one at the present moment? The Most High is with you. If you remain in the secret place of God's presence, you will be like Joshua and Caleb. They were strong and brave and able to go in and take the country and to possess the land, even though they were the oldest of all those going in.

The Most High blessed Ruth Gardiner with a long life. I came to live in Mom's house to care for her at Easter of 2014. She had turned 100 the previous November. I took a leave of absence from my receptionist job at Auburn Hills Christian Center. The timing was just right. For years, I would always remind Mom, "You have sown care so you will reap care in your life." I didn't know that her caregiver would be me! I came in April and in December my husband retired from his position in pastoral care at Auburn Hills Christian Center and we both took care of Mom in her home. Before he retired, we got together on most weekends. I would drive to the east side of the state, or Tony would travel to Grand Rapids.

Mom was an avid reader so she was sharp as a tack. She loved playing the organ and she drove a car until she was 95. The hardest thing about not driving was losing her independence. She had to rely on other people to take her grocery shopping. She did take the "Go Bus" or a taxi to get around to various events in the city.

When I arrived, I became her taxi. I took her to the grocery store and to garage sales which were so much fun for her. We played Scrabble a lot and I would beat her and feel a little guilty, just a little. The next night she would beat me and we would laugh. She went for walks using a walker and would say to me: Honey, I have to keep moving.

My mother, Ruth Gardiner, joyfully returned to her Maker and we had a wonderful family reunion to celebrate her life.

Mom always commented that she so enjoyed having a family and that she would love to have all five of her children all over again. She felt that she had not done a good enough job mothering them, and she said that she had learned so much over the years, surely she would do a much better job the second time around. God's thoughts are higher than ours. Mom did her best and the Lord saw her caring heart and how she trusted in Him. She bowed her knee to Him every night. He blessed her with long life and showed her His salvation.

There were so many wonderful people involved in Jim's care. Mom wrote these words for her obituary: "Ruth thanks everyone who helped to provide for Coach Jim Gardiner's needs for thirty-seven years."

In closing, God answers prayer three ways: yes, no, and wait. If Joshua and Caleb could wait forty years to enter the Promised Land, we can be greatly encouraged by their example when we are waiting for God to move in our circumstances.

The decision is announced by messengers, the holy ones declare the verdict, so that the living may know that the Most High *is sovereign over all kingdoms on earth and gives them to anyone he wishes and sets over them the lowliest of people.—Daniel 4:17*

Chapter 12
Pray and Process

Add your own prayers below.

Adoration: Most High, I love you because...

Confession: Lord Jesus, I have blown it...

Thanksgiving: Almighty God, I thank you for...

Supplication: Holy Spirit of the living God...

Process What You Have Learned

1. When has God said yes to your prayers?

2. When has God said no to your prayers?

3. When has God told you to wait?

4. What are you asking God for right now?

Bibliography

All Scripture quotations, unless otherwise indicated, are taken from *The Holy Bible, New International Version* (NIV). Copyright ©1973, 1978, 1984, 2011 by Biblica, Inc. Used by permission of Zondervan. All rights reserved worldwide. www.zondervan.com

www.biblegateway.com

www.blueletterbible.org,

Dake, Finis Jennings. *Dake's Annotated Reference Bible.* Lawrenceville, GA: Dake Publishing, 1963.

Graham, Billy. "July 10: I Will Look unto the Hills—Covered by Christ." *Unto the Hills: A Daily Devotional.* Word Publishing, Dallas, TX.1986

Spurgeon, Charles H. *The Treasury of David.* Vol. 2. Peabody, MA: Hendrickson Publishers, 1988.

Strong, James. *Strong's Exhaustive Concordance of the Bible.* Authorized King James Version Text. McLean, VA: MacDonald Publishing Company. 1973

Tenney, Merrill C., ed. *The Zondervan Pictorial Encyclopedia of the Bible.* Vol. 4. Pp 720-721; J.B. Scott; Regency Reference Library. The Zondervan Corporation, Grand Rapids, MI 1975–76.

Made in the USA
Lexington, KY
12 August 2019